Series on Grey System

This series aims to publish books on grey system and various applications in the fields of natural sciences, social sciences and engineering.

This series is devoted to the international advancement of the theory and application of grey system. It seeks to foster professional exchanges between scientists and practitioners who are interested in the models, methods and applications of grey system. Through the pioneering work completed over 40 years, grey data analysis methods have become powerful tools in addressing system with poor information.

Books published with this series will explore the models and applications of grey system, in order to tackle poor information more effectively and efficiently. The series aims to provide state-of-the-art information and case studies on new developments and trends in grey system research and its potential application to solve practical problems.

Coverage includes, but is not limited to:

- Foundations of grey systems theory
- Grey sequence operators
- Grey relational analysis models
- Grey clustering evaluations models
- Techniques for grey system forecasting
- Grey models for decision-making
- Combined grey models
- Grey input-output models
- Techniques for grey control
- Various applications of grey system models in the fields of natural sciences, social sciences and engineering.

Rafał Mierzwiak

Methodological Aspects of Grey Systems Theory in Management Research

Springer

Rafał Mierzwiak
Poznań University of Technology
Poznań, Poland

ISSN 2731-4936 ISSN 2731-4944 (electronic)
Series on Grey System
ISBN 978-981-97-2412-3 ISBN 978-981-97-2413-0 (eBook)
https://doi.org/10.1007/978-981-97-2413-0

This Springer imprint is published by the registered company Springer Nature Singapore Pte Ltd.
The registered company address is: 152 Beach Road, #21-01/04 Gateway East, Singapore 189721, Singapore

Preface

This book is a summary of the research that I have had the opportunity to conduct under grant no. 2018M630561; supported by the China Postdoctoral Science Foundation and through the support provided by the Nanjing University of Aeronautics and Astronautics under project no. 2017-F-09-01006. Furthermore, my research has been and continues to be supported by statutory grants from the Poznań University of Technology.

This book would never have been written without the many people who have left their mark on my academic path. In the first instance, I would like to express special thanks to my mentors. The first of these is Prof. Władyslaw Mantura, who was the supervisor of my doctoral thesis and at the same time for many years the head of the department in which I had the honour of working at Poznań University of Technology. The second person to whom I extend my sincere thanks is Prof. Sifeng Liu, director of the Institute for Grey Systems Study at the Nanjing University of Aeronautics and Astronautics, where I had the honour of doing my postdoctoral training. I would also like to thank my colleagues who, through many inspiring discussions, helped to clarify many of the concepts presented in this book. In particular, I would like to thank my colleagues from the Poznań University of Technology. Prof. Ewa Więcek-Janka, Dr. Joanna Majchrzak, and Dr. Marcin Nowak. I would also like to thank my colleagues at the Nanjing University of Aeronautics and Astronautics for their invaluable assistance, in particular Prof. Naiming Xie, Prof. Chuanmin Mi, Dr. Wenjie Dong, Dr. Tao Liam, and Dr. Ehsan Javanmardi. I would also like to thank Prof. Yingjie Yang of De Montfort University, Leicester, and to mention the late Prof. Czesław Cempel, a pioneer and populariser of grey systems theory research, in whose research methodology lecture I first had the opportunity to encounter and familiarise myself with the theory. It is impossible to mention the wide range of colleagues who have been kind to me. To all of them and to each of them individually, I would also like to say: thank you!

A separate word of thanks goes to my daughter and wife for their support, for their love, for everything!

Poznań, Poland Rafał Mierzwiak

Introduction

The aim of the research presented in this monograph was to develop basic assumptions related to the application of grey systems theory in research conducted in the management sciences. Taking into account the aim of the research set in this way, the results of this research can be reduced to a set of methodological guidelines for the selection and application of grey analytical methods in the field of research in management sciences. The object of consideration is therefore the research process, its specifics, and the structure that currently prevails in research in this scientific discipline. The main research aspect, from the angle of which the analysis of such a defined research object was conducted, was the modelling of uncertainty using grey systems theory in quantitative research conducted for the practical and cognitive use of management sciences. The aim of this book thus requires an answer to the following main research problem: How to reconstruct the research paradigm of grey systems theory in order to make it useful in the management sciences? The answer to this question will make it possible to fill the cognitive gap, which can be reduced to the following statement: In grey systems theory there is a poorly recognised problem of its adaptation to the requirements of the methodology of social sciences such as management science. The validity of this issue is important insofar as grey methods are increasingly being used in this type of research, and difficulties in justifying their use can be identified at a methodological level. Typically, these justifications are based on general statements, analogies, and intuitions, without reference to rational, logical, and deductive premises.

In view of the main research problem formulated in this way, the main objective of the research, and the outlined research gap, it is necessary to answer the following specific questions:

Q1: What are the reasons for grey information in management science research?
Q2: What is the relevance of the axiomatic account of grey in the applications of grey methods in management science?
Q3: What are the similarities between the systems approach in grey systems theory and in management science?

Q4: What is the potential of grey methods in research strategies and research paradigms in management science?
Q5: To what extent is the potential of grey systems theory currently being exploited in management science research?
Q6: How, at the level of methodological soundness, do you enhance the applicability of grey systems theory in management science?

Answering this set of specific questions requires two important assumptions. First, the discussion assumes that management science is a social science. It goes without saying that they also draw on the achievements of the technical or natural sciences, but this should not change the basic social dimension of the discipline. Secondly, as grey systems theory is intended as an analytical methodology to support research processes in the management sciences, the aim of the discussion is to reconstruct, adapt, and reinterpret the formalism of grey systems theory in terms of social science methodology. The reverse process, i.e. a strenuous effort to make management research problems and methods similar to those found in the natural, technical, or mathematical sciences, is not the aim.

The aim of the research and the structure of the research questions, as well as the researcher's assumptions, are reflected in the content structure of the following chapters.

In Chap. 1, considerations are focused on proving the following research statements.

S1: The reason for the presence of grey information in management science research stems directly from the complexity of information-decision processes in management systems and the associated limitations of quantification procedures relevant to research in the neopositivist-functionalist-system paradigm that dominates management.
S2: Grey uncertainty modelled axiomatically using grey space introduces criteria for demarcation between grey systems theory and other approaches to uncertainty modelling, and therefore, facilitates the delineation of the use of grey methods in management in this way.
S3: The systems approach in management is incompatible and incomparable with that taken in grey systems theory, which, however, does not entail negative implications associated with the use of grey methods in research in this field.
S4: Grey systems theory methods are mainly used in research conducted in the neo-positivist-functionalist-systems paradigm and in research strategies where we have a low level of control of the variables under study, aiming to reproduce the realism of the context, with a medium level of generalisability of the results.

This chapter first discusses the issue of quantification procedures in research. They were related to the difficulty of quantifying the complexity of information and decision-making flows in management systems. As a result of the considerations, the relationship between quantification and the ability to identify and express grey information is indicated. The chapter then goes on to discuss the issue of grey space as the author's axiomatisation of grey systems theory. The problem of delimitation is addressed and related to the extent to which grey methods can find application in management research. Following this issue, the chapter undertakes a methodological reflection on the issues of paradigms and research agendas in management, taking into account the assumption that management science should be methodologically assigned to the social sciences. Through an analysis of research paradigms and strategies, the relationship between them and the methodological assumptions of grey systems theory is indicated.

Chapter 2 focuses on developing the issues from Chap. 1 in terms of analysing the potential of particular groups of methods in management research. Methodological issues of grey numbers, relationship analysis models, predictive models, and decision models are shown and discussed in detail. This chapter supports and develops chapter one in the context of confirming research statement S3. This compositional procedure in the structure of the content is the result of adopting a general to specific approach as the overarching logical order of the theoretical research carried out.

Chapter 3 focuses on justifying the following research statement:

S5: Grey systems theory models in management research are hybrid in nature, the result of integration with other data analysis methods.

To provide a multifaceted analysis to support the research statement made, a systematic review of the literature was carried out that focused on this issue. The results of this analysis, together with the entire methodology, are shown in detail in this chapter.

Chapter 4 focuses on justifying the following research statement:

S6: Algorithmisation of the process of selecting grey methods in research significantly organises this issue methodologically, and thus increases the application potential of grey systems theory in management research.

The chapter designed algorithms for the selection of grey methods in research. This was done by synthesising the considerations of the earlier chapters, which reconstructed the research paradigm of grey systems theory in order to adapt it to research in the management sciences. In addition to substantiating S6's statement, this chapter finalises the main objective of the thesis and fills an identified research gap.

The research shown in this monograph is theoretical in nature and methodological in nature. Therefore, in the research process, research questions (Q1–Q6) were posed and then corresponding research statements (S1–S6) were formulated instead of hypotheses. The research statement was subjected to verification and justification. Statements S1–S4 were verified using the method of critical analysis of the literature and the method of analysis and logical construction. These methods are a manifestation of the deductive way of thinking adopted in the research process. Statement S5 was verified by a systematic literature survey, while statement S6 was verified by synthesising the results of previous considerations and conclusions from the process of designing guidelines for the grey research method selection model in the context of management research.

Contents

About the Author

Rafał Mierzwiak currently works at the Faculty of Management Engineering, Poznań University of Technology, where he heads the Laboratory of Quantitative Methods and Grey Systems. His research interests include the application of grey systems theory in management and quality sciences, taking into account methodological and epistemological issues. He actively collaborates with the most important scientific centres in the field of grey systems theory. He currently serves as Deputy Secretary General for the International Association of Grey Systems and Uncertainty and is a member of The IEEE Systems, Man, and Cybernetics Society (SMCS)—TC on Grey Systems. He has repeatedly participated in international conferences where he presented his research in plenary sessions. His papers and research articles have also received numerous awards from the grey systems theory research community. He has participated in many international research projects. As a postdoctoral fellowship, he led a project funded by the China Postdoctoral Science Foundation conducted at the Institute for Grey Systems Study at Nanjing University of Aeronautics and Astronautics.

Chapter 1
The Category of Grey in Management Science Research

1.1 Grey Systems Theory as a New Methodology for Quantitative Modelling of Uncertainty in Management Science Research

The essence of all management functions is the implementation of information and decision-making processes. The main element of a manager's work, therefore, is making accurate decisions. A typical decision-making process related to the specifics of management can be divided into the following stages [1, 2]:

- Structure the decision problem; The outcome of this step should be a clear description of the situation requiring management action;
- The identification of a set of relevant objectives and requirements by an individual, team, or group that is a decision-maker and actor in the decision-making process in the organisation. The outcome of this stage should be the formulation of decision criteria;
- Search for alternatives for solving the formulated decision problem; the result of this step should be a set of possible action scenarios;
- The act of choice should result in the adoption of the optimal solution option on the basis of the decision criteria formulated and then communicate it within the organisation; The extent of this communication should be appropriate to the extent of the consequences resulting from the decision option adopted;
- Implementation of the decision, the essence of which is the appropriate choice of measures and actions aimed at effective implementation of the adopted solution. A very important element of this stage should be the identification of possible problems related to the implementation of the decision; of course, at earlier stages this problem is considered; however, it is often the implementation stage that

The original version of the chapter has been revised. A correction to this chapter can be found at https://doi.org/10.1007/978-981-97-2413-0_5

R. Mierzwiak, *Methodological Aspects of Grey Systems Theory in Management Research*, Series on Grey System, https://doi.org/10.1007/978-981-97-2413-0_1

brings to light problems not previously considered during the act of selecting the optimal option; hence, this stage may end up returning to the decision selection stage or even, in the face of new knowledge acquired during an unsuccessful implementation attempt, to the options search stage;
- A review of the decision, the purpose of which is to check the effectiveness of the decision taken, to introduce possible corrections and improvement actions; a frequent result of this stage may also be a rethinking of the structure of the objectives adopted and the requirements set by the organisation.

As can be seen, the decision-making process is designed to adapt the organisation to existing conditions and constraints by selecting a set of optimal and possible actions. An additional effect of this process is the acquisition of knowledge in action by decision makers, which is fundamental in reducing uncertainty and risk in the functioning of the organisation.

Risk and uncertainty are inherent features of any human activity, including decision-making processes in organisations. In essence, we can identify the concept of uncertainty as the conscious state of the subject of the decision-making process in which he or she cannot determine the important consequences of the decision he or she is making or is unable to identify the important features of those consequences. The concept of risk, on the other hand, we can define as a state in which the subject of the decision-making process is able to relatively identify the consequences of his decision and predict the possibility of their occurrence, and is able to quantitatively characterise and describe them. Simplistically, therefore, we can say that risk is that part of uncertainty that lends itself to some form of quantification.

On the one hand, we can relate the concept of uncertainty in management to issues related to the activity of managers and the decision-making processes in which they are involved, but the aspect related to the research and analytical perspective in management science is also important. In the managerial and practical activity perspective, modelling data uncertainty in the context of methods that support rational decision-making is extremely important. However, in the cognitive perspective, data uncertainty is fundamental to scientific inference in management science.

The literature identifies various causes of uncertainty modelling problems, among which the most common are errors in the data collection process, inadequacy of the adopted research instruments and data collection methodology, and difficulties in quantifying the linguistic characteristics of the phenomenon or object under study ([3], p. 7). Analysed in more depth, we can essentially reduce all these problems to the issue of proper quantification of the features describing the phenomenon or object in question. Of course, such a statement does not exclude or negate the importance of qualitative research; however, adopting a neo-positivist research paradigm, the target state in the research process should be a quantitative approach, which in the context of uncertainty modelling manifests itself in the issue of quantification.

Quantification, in the most general sense, can be called a set of steps aimed at providing quantitative data for the purpose of induction [4]. In terms of the general theory of quality (qualtitology), quantification is understood as the attribution of a given attribute of some object of analysis, a quantitative characteristic ([5], p. 56).

However, it is not resolved whether such an attribution is meaningful in the induction process.

Among the basic methods of quantification in management science, we can include: measurement, scaling, construction of indicators [6]. Measurement applies to physical characteristics that are directly observable, while scaling or indicator construction apply to abstract characteristics that are not directly observable in physical reality.

The problem of measuring real objects is dealt with by measurement theory. Its essence boils down to the search for the mapping of empirical relations identified in reality into an appropriate symbolic system of a numerical nature. In order to formally express this thought, let us assume that

- $X = x_1, x_2 \ldots x_n$—set of empirical observables
- f—characteristic to be measured
- φ—any relationship that orders a set of observables in terms of a measured characteristic f
- (X, φ)—empirical relational system
- R—set of real numbers

By adopting these designations, the measurement of a feature of a f of a given object is understood to be the following function:

$$\Pi : (X, \varphi) \to R$$

Measurement therefore maps the empirical relational system into a set of real numbers. The fundamental problem associated with this mapping is the issue of representation. It boils down to the fact that measurement is possible and meaningful when there is a homomorphism between the empirical system and the set of real numbers. This homomorphism occurs when a certain relation φ is preserved and exists in the set of real numbers R.

The characterisation of the existing homomorphism between the empirical and numerical systems allows the following four basic measurement scales to be identified [7]:

- in the case where the homomorphism only preserves the equivalence relation, then we have a nominal measurement scale by which comparisons of the type can be made: x_1 is different from x_2 or x_1 is identical to x_2;
- in the case where the homomorphism preserves the partial order relation, then we have an ordinal measurement scale, thanks to which, in addition to the comparisons characteristic of the nominal scale, we can make comparisons of the type: x_1 is greater than x_2 or x_1 is not worse than x_2;
- if the homomorphism preserves the order and the proportion of differences between the measurements, then we have an interval measurement scale, thanks to which, in addition to the comparisons characteristic of the nominal and ordinal scales, we can also make comparisons of the following type: x_1 is greater by a given value than x_2,

- if the homomorphism preserves the relations between measurements, then we have a quotient measurement scale, thanks to which, in addition to the comparisons characteristic of the nominal, ordinal and interval scales, we can also make comparisons of the following type: x_1 is greater by a certain number of times than x_2.

Ordinal and nominal scales are among the scales that provide data on which, from a formal point of view, arithmetic operations such as addition, subtraction, division, and multiplication cannot be meaningfully performed. Operations of addition and subtraction are possible for data on at least the interval scale, while the additional operations of multiplication and division are possible for data expressed on the quotient scale.

Measurement in the sense proposed by measurement theories is adequate to measure phenomena of a physical nature. This view of measurement is of limited use in the social sciences, such as management or economics. It does not cover the complex and not directly observable theoretical constructs used in the construction of research processes in these sciences. Hence, for the use of the social sciences, measurement procedures are not just a simple assignment of numbers to some objects according to certain rules but more of a bridge connecting theoretical constructs to the observable empirical world. One of the most common and developed approaches to measurement in this way is what is known as scaling.

Scaling is linked to one of the more commonly used research techniques in the management sciences, namely research using survey questionnaires. Here, the process of scaling involves coding survey responses with numbers and then using analytical rules to assign, to the state of the characteristic being measured, a position on an assumed numerical continuum, which we call the measurement scale. It should be noted that while in measurement theory the measurement scale results from the property of homomorphism between the empirical and theoretical systems, in the scaling procedure the scale is the effect of the choice of the numerical continuum to which the states of the characteristics of the object or phenomenon under study will be related. When we are dealing with survey research, these characteristics states are approximated by questionnaire questions.

One of the best-known scaling methods is the one proposed by Likert. It is also often referred to as the summative scaling method. In this method, in order to measure a characteristic, a set of questions is formulated for the respondent, and the answers are coded using natural numbers. The results are then summed and averaged. This yields a position on the measurement scale. The quality of measurement by means of Likert scaling is related to the relevance of the questions asked and the reliability, which can be measured by the reliability coefficient of the *Cronbach* coefficient.

Another way of scaling is the method proposed by Guttman, which is often referred to as scalogram analysis. Like Likert summative scaling, it also uses a survey questionnaire. This questionnaire contains a series of questions related to the individual characteristics being measured. The respondent answers them dichotomously, either agreeing or disagreeing with the statement in question. It is important that the questions are logically linked to each other and arranged in such a way that if the answer to a question is yes, the next questions in the questionnaire should also be answered in the affirmative. In the event that the respondent answers differently, however, either the respondent is making a mistake or the questions have been poorly formulated and arranged. We assume here, of course, a rational action of the respondent in the survey process. The quality of measurement by the Guttman scaling is linked to the relevance of the questions asked and the reliability, which can be measured by the Guttman's coefficient of reproducibility.

Scaling is a very popular and useful procedure in many social science studies. Hence, one can see a continuous development of methodologies in this field. This is perhaps most evident in research in psychology, whose focus is the analysis of abstract traits. In psychology, an entire branch of psychology called psychometrics deals with this issue. Psychometric research at the level of data collection can resemble the Likert approach. The similarity arises from the use of survey questionnaires as the primary measurement instrument. However, the collected data is analysed in a more sophisticated way than simple summative scaling. Furthermore, in contrast to the Likert approach, the psychometric approach seeks to justify the measurement and anchor it methodologically in some broader theoretical concept.

The construction of synthetic evaluation indicators is also a very popular method of quantification. This idea is most firmly rooted in economics, where a number of indicators are developed and published to characterise the state of the economy. However, this does not exclude the usefulness of this approach in management. On the contrary, in many cases, the indicator approach is used to monitor key aspects of an organisation. The construction of indicators is based, in the most general sense, on measuring the quality of some object or phenomenon. The procedure for this measurement involves the operation of assigning a set of characteristics to a given object of analysis. This set is then subjected to appropriate systematisation so that the prescribed characteristics are appropriately grouped together and the analytical capacity of the whole procedure is thus increased. The basic problem in this type of methodology is the appropriate identification of features, which should take into account the following criteria ([5], p. 93):

- the amount of information contained in the trait formula,
- the constitutivity of a feature, i.e. the extent to which a feature illustrates the distinctiveness of an object from other objects,
- objectivity and credibility characteristics,
- nonduplication of information about the object contained in other features,
- The research and design tradition of a particular discipline of science or practice,
- the difficulty of identifying and observing a feature (availability of the feature),
- accuracy and precision of the feature as a source of information about the object.

Furthermore, an important element in the construction of synthetic indicators is the solution to the problem of comparability of the denominators of the characteristics under study and the issues related to their aggregation. These issues are in the field of interest of statistical research and are also, at the general methodological level, an important issue in qualitative research [5, 8–12].

The complexity of the object of management research and the interdisciplinary nature of issues related to management processes in organisations mean that a high level of uncertain information is generated in research procedures and practical activities in the management sciences. Attempts to manage this uncertainty require the use of procedures of the aforementioned quantification such as measurement, scaling, or the construction of indicators. Within each of these procedures, information can take different forms. It can be probabilistic, fuzzy, or grey information. Each of these forms has peculiar analytical methodologies that must be taken into account in the aforementioned quantification procedures.

The probabilistic approach undoubtedly has the longest research tradition and is firmly established in the scientific world. The fundamental concept in probabilistics is probability. Its definition is now axiomatic and based on probabilistic space [13]. However, this is not the only interpretation of the concept of probability known in the literature. In general, however, the common denominator is that the concept of probability is the result of adopting the logic of inductive inference [14–17]. The probabilistic view of uncertainty modelling has found many applications; however, it also has limitations. Probabilistic methods mostly assume certain distributions of random variables that describe the phenomena under analysis. In reality, the analysed variables may not fulfil the theoretical assumptions. In addition, there is the problem of the level of measurement of variables, which is particularly important in social sciences such as management. There, we are usually dealing with characteristics that can at most be measured on an ordinal scale. Consequently, many probabilistic methods, e.g. all statistical parametric methods, can be used to a limited extent.

The fuzzy approach to uncertainty is based on a generalisation of classical set theory [18]. In fuzzy logic, an element can only belong to a set to a certain extent and not definitively, as is the case in classical set theory. This belonging is mapped by means of a membership function. It allows for the formal modelling of vague concepts resulting from imprecision in natural language. Its classical applications are decision support and the mathematical formalisation of linguistic variables. Despite the many successful practical applications of fuzzy logic, attention should also be drawn to its weaknesses. Among the most important of these are that the selection of membership functions is arbitrary and that performing successive operations on fuzzy quantities increases the level of uncertainty in the analysis.

The grey approach is one of the latest approaches to uncertainty modelling. It is undoubtedly a collection of very diverse analytical methods with a systemic pedigree on the one hand, and on the other hand, like fuzzy logic or probabilistic approaches, it refers to classical set theory. Historically, one of the earliest works on the subject, which we today refer to as grey system theory, is the work on multivalued algebra [19]. Multivalued algebra in its main ideas is in many places identical to operations on the constructs we today call grey numbers. As with the grey numbers mentioned above, its basic property is that it defines a set of mathematical operations and transformations on numbers about which we know only that they are between known limits. In the case of multivalued algebra, as in the case of grey numbers, the element on which the operations are performed is an unknown number within a known interval, not the interval itself. The idea behind both approaches is essentially the same. However, the differences become apparent at the level of mathematical notation and the research objectives behind the development of the two concepts. In the case of grey systems theory, this objective was of a utilitarian nature related to cybernetic modelling, whereas in the case of multivalued algebra, it was a typically cognitive objective related to the precise and formal description of a new algebraic system.

Multivalued algebra is therefore a typical theoretical construct classified as pure mathematics. It can be of theoretical and historical importance for grey systems theory. The theoretical solutions adopted in it can still inspire research and enrich research in improving the algebraic system of grey numbers today.

The actual development of grey systems theory can be dated back to the research conducted by Deng [20, 21]. These focused on modelling uncertainty in control processes of systems with incomplete information. The perspective and context of this research was related to issues of the methodological foundations of cybernetic engineering. Accordingly, grey-box analogies were introduced to clarify the concept of grey, referring to the well-known white-box and black-box concepts in cybernetics. In this initial stage of the development of grey systems theory, a datological understanding of information was implicitly adopted. The category of information was treated as an attribute of reality rather than as an attribute of the process of human cognition. This was the result of the engineering and technical pedigree of the theory of grey systems. However, this did not prevent the rather dynamic and rapid development of research of an applied nature in social, economic, or management issues [22–24]. Nowadays, one can even put forward the following thesis: the dominant direction of research work in the field of grey systems theory is practical applications concerning phenomena at the borderline between engineering and social sciences. Furthermore, by analysing the dominant trends in methodological and epistemological issues in grey systems theory, one can undoubtedly conclude that there has been a significant change in the approach to the category of information. Information, as in the social sciences, is approached infologically. It is treated as part of the process of human cognition of reality. On the contrary, the category of uncertainty is treated as a result of human cognitive limitations.

Today, grey systems theories can be seen as a new approach to modelling uncertainty about the applicability to interdisciplinary and complex research and practical problems, such as those most often encountered in management. This practical dimension is currently the most frequently addressed in grey systems theory publications. This is because, during the period of dynamic development of such a young knowledge discipline, the emphasis was on the development of a number of application tools that constituted, on the one hand, the validity and, on the other hand, the usefulness of grey systems theory in research and business practice. Hence, what seems symptomatic of relatively young knowledge disciplines is the occurrence of an imbalance between the development of the theory's application tools and its philosophical foundations, particularly in the ontological and epistemological fields.

The development of grey systems theory is strongly influenced and permeated by other theoretical approaches and concepts with a longer research tradition, such as the already mentioned probability theory and fuzzy logic, but also rough set theory, cybernetics and systems theory. The aforementioned theories and analytical approaches provide a benchmark of methodological demarcation for grey systems theory, and in many cases, also a benchmark of methodological correctness.

A generally accepted criterion that distinguishes grey systems theory from other uncertainty modelling methods is the ability to descript, explore, and predict many phenomena without having a large information base. The theory is assumed to be suitable for the analysis of incomplete, sparse, and incomplete data, and where the mechanisms governing the phenomena under analysis are only partially known. The criterion adopted in this way makes it possible to distinguish the application domain of grey systems theory from typical statistical methods, where a large dataset of the phenomenon being analysed is required. However, in the case of fuzzy logic, the criterion of a small number of data is not a sufficiently delimiter from grey system theory. Thus, it can be concluded that fuzzy logic or set theory is complementary in applications to grey systems theory, given the number of data required for analysis. The differences in applications are only due to the structure and the way the data are organised and represented.

1.2 Selected Methodological Problems of Grey Systems Theory and Their Relevance to Management Science Research

The most important methodological challenge of grey systems theory is the attempt to define the concept of grey information. In most cases, analogies and pictorial descriptions are used to discuss this concept without a strict and formal definition. Intuitively, such an account may be sufficient, but epistemologically it cannot form the basis for any scientific theory.

One of the most commonly used analogies to explain the concept of grey and grey information is the concept referring to the cybernetic "black" and "white box" In this approach, the assumption is made that if we have a given system about which we are only able to make a judgement that the system exists but we have no knowledge of its structure, behaviour, boundaries, relations within it and elements, we call such a system a "black system" and information about it "black information". Conversely, if we have complete and exhaustive information about the analysed system, we call such a system a "white system", and information about it a "white information". On the other hand, in the case of an intermediate state, when we are dealing with a system about which we have only partial knowledge, incomplete and incomplete, we speak of a "grey system" and "grey information" [25]. The grey system is thus the result of a dialectical unification between a system about which the cognitive subject has full, complete and certain information and a system about which the cognitive subject has no knowledge.

In an illustrative manner, the idea discussed is usually represented in the literature as in Fig. 1.1 ([26], p. 574).

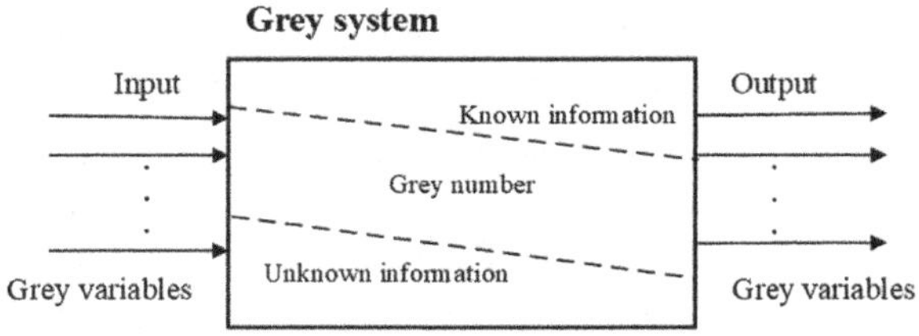

Fig. 1.1 The idea of a grey system in cybernetic terms

Most of the literature explaining the essence of the concept of a grey system assumes that its basic elements are variables expressed by grey numbers. In grey systems theory, a grey number is a concrete real number about which we know only that it falls within a certain range. The arithmetic operations performed on grey numbers constitute one of the most important and fundamental sections of grey systems theory [27], pp. 23–28, [28–31]. However, narrowing the grey systems theory to the issue of grey numbers omits many important research areas of the theory. Consequently, a concept based on the analogy of cybernetic 'black box' and 'white box' cannot constitute a general and universal grey system theoretical concept.

The criticisms formulated can be a starting point for an in-depth consideration of the methodological foundations of grey systems theory, which would allow the logical integration of a diverse set of issues into a single research programme. One way of such integration is to attempt to formulate the most basic and initial methodological rules. Such an approach is intended as an attempt to axiomatise the issue. The most notorious set of axioms consists of: ([32, 33], pp. 14–18):

- Axiom of Informational Differences. The "difference" implies the existence of information. Each piece of information must carry some kind of "difference".
- Axiom of non-uniqueness. The solution to any problem with incomplete and indeterminate information is not unique.
- Minimal Information Axiom. One characteristic of grey system theory is that it makes the most and best use of the "minimal amount of available information."
- Axiom of the recognition base. Information is the foundation on which people recognise and understand (nature).
- Axiom of the New Information Priority. The function of new pieces of information is greater than that of old pieces of information.
- Axiom of Absolute Greyness. The "incompleteness" of the information is absolute. Incompleteness and nondeterminism of information have generality.

Analysing the content of the axioms presented, the following few criticisms arise.

- First, it can be questioned that they are axioms in the logical sense on which a deductive system of assertions can be built; rather, they have the character of general principles, induced from practical reflections on the study of uncertainty;
- Second, these axioms do not indicate the accepted viewpoint on the ontological structure of reality, and therefore the resulting epistemological assumptions;
- Thirdly, the axioms introduced are not a sufficient demarcation criterion for grey systems theory from other methods of modelling uncertainty, as they are mainly

concerned with the general nature of information uncertainty and not only with its specific variety, which grey systems theory deals with.

The resolution of these problems may come from the development of the philosophical foundations of grey system theory. Essentially, there are now two main approaches to this issue. The first locates the epistemology of grey systems theory in the post-modern current [34, 35]. The second is an approach that refers to analytic philosophy [25, 36, 37]. Regardless of the approach adopted, however, their common denominator is to point out that grey systems theory is a methodology whose scope of application is greater the greater the level of uncertainty in its structure and behaviour that is analysed [38]. In turn, this uncertainty is related to the level of complexity of the system under analysis. Figure 1.2 illustrates the usefulness of grey systems theory in modelling the uncertainty of systems with different specifications. Systems with the lowest level of complexity are formal systems, commonly found in sciences such as logic or mathematics. At a higher level of complexity, and therefore cognitive difficulty, are technical systems. Systems of the highest complexity, on the other hand, are praxeological systems, i.e. those whose main component is acting humans. This class of systems includes systems in which management science has as its object of interest. Learning about such systems involves the greatest difficulty and the sheer level of uncertainty with which they are burdened is the greatest. Uncertainty in this type of system is often due to information gaps (incomplete information), a small amount of information about the systems being learnt, and the inability to model uncertainty using specific numerical values (imprecise information).

When comparing grey systems theory with probabilistic or fuzzy approaches, it is important to note that there is little ongoing research in grey systems theory that refers to classical set theory. The concept of grey is usually explained by analogy

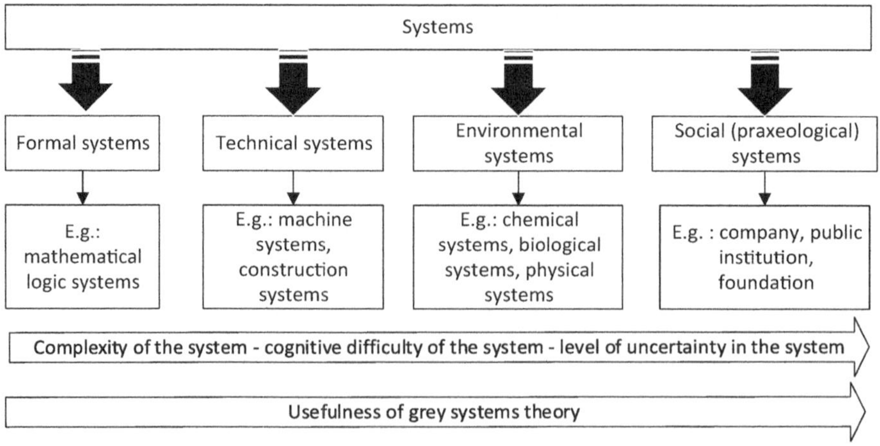

Fig. 1.2 Classification of systems according to complexity and the usefulness of grey systems theory in their modelling

without adequate formalisation. Exceptions include studies in which the initial theoretical construct is a 'portion of grey information' [27], pp. 14–15). However, the cited studies do not aim to develop the theoretical underpinnings of grey systems theory, only to conduct a comparative analysis of this theory in the context of other approaches to uncertainty modelling. However, this does not change the fact that by modifying them and adding additional elements, it is possible to propose an axiomatic definition of grey. One proposal for such a modification is to propose an axiomatisation of the concept of greyness using grey space [25]. The concept of grey space was inspired by the analogy to probabilistic space.

Classical set theory was adopted as the basis for the axiomatisation of grey system theory. A grey space is understood as a triple $\left\{\Omega, \mathcal{F}, G^{\circ}\right\}$, where:

- Ω denotes the set which is the analysis space,
- $\mathcal{F}$ will be a σ - algebra generated on the set of Ω, i.e.: $\emptyset \in \mathcal{F}$ and $A \in \mathcal{F} \Rightarrow A' \in \mathcal{F}$and $A_1, A_2, A_3 \in \mathcal{F} \Rightarrow \cup_{i=1}^{\infty} A_i \in \mathcal{F}$,
- G° will be the function that maps $\mathcal{F}$ into a set of real numbers, which formally can be written $G^{\circ} : \mathcal{F} \to$ R and will be a grey function when it satisfies the four axioms:

Axiom 1. $G^{\circ}\ (A_i) \geq 0$ for any $A_i \in \mathcal{F}$.

Axiom 2. $G^{\circ}\ (A_i) = 0 \Leftrightarrow A_i = \{a_i\}$, whereby $A_i = \{a_i\}$ denotes any one-element set belonging to $\mathcal{F}$.

Axiom 3. $G^{\circ}\ (\Omega) = 1$.

Axiom 4. $G^{\circ}\ (\cup_{i \in N} A_i) = \sum\limits_{i \in N} G^{\circ}(A_i)$, where: $A_i \cap A_j = \emptyset \wedge A_i \neq \{a_i\}$.

The set Ω denoting the analysis space can also be called the set of possible events or the set of possible realisations of some variable (whose exact value is not known, but the set/interval in which this number is located is known). The set Ω is not interpreted at the same time as in the case of probability theory, because the events analysed in the case of the grey space concept are not random in nature.

The collection $\mathcal{F}$ is $\sigma-$ algebra generated on the set Ω. The set has three key properties:

- To the set $\mathcal{F}$ belongs the empty set ($\emptyset$),
- If a certain set A belongs to $\mathcal{F}$, then the set $\mathcal{F}$ also belongs to the complement of the set $A(A')$,
- If certain sets belong to $\mathcal{F}$, then the set which is the sum of these sets also belongs to $\mathcal{F}$.

A formalisation using $\sigma-$ algebra has a profound justification. If we can specify the grey level for a set, then we should also be able to specify the grey level of its complement. Furthermore, if we are able to specify the grey level for the sum of sets, then we should also be able to indicate the grey level for each set separately.

The formalisations presented of the concept of greyness result from its intuitive understanding. Grey in intuitive terms is the uncertainty of information resulting from the fact that a subject in the process of cognition can only say about an element that it belongs to some subset of the space of analysis.

To better illustrate the concept of analysis space, it is useful to use the following example ([25], pp. 204–205):

- Suppose that the space of analysis is the height among adults in a population and assume that the lowest person in the population is 150 cm and the highest is 220 cm; hence $\Omega = [150, 220]$;
- Let us assume that we are able to determine that an individual in this population who is of interest to us has a height between 180 and 190 cm; we do not know exactly what this value is, we only know that it is within this range;
- The information we have on a selected individual in a given population is called grey information defined over the height range found in the population, namely: between 150 and 220 cm.

The association of the grey categories with the analysis space has a profound rationale. It can be illustrated as follows: grey with analysis space; we estimate for costing purposes the price of some product and consider it to be between \$180 and \$190, using in the estimation the knowledge of the current state of the market and the fact that historically the market price has been between \$50 and \$200. Now, comparing this example with the earlier growth example, we can see that the difference between the upper and lower limits is the same in both cases. However, the information in the case of the price for costing purposes, given its possible range of variation, is more precise. This reference to the size of the space on which the analysis is performed makes it important not only to estimate upper and lower limits, but also to estimate the order of magnitude on which these operations are performed.

From the proposed axioms, it follows that the grey level function is a nonnegative function, which for one-element sets takes the value 0. Such an assumption is not objectionable, since if we indicate a one-element set in the analysis space, this is the same as indicating unambiguously which element we mean. Hence, the grey level should take the smallest possible value, i.e. 0.

Axiom 4 introducing the prohibition of additive convertibility for the case of the sum of one-element sets requires a wider comment. The rationale behind this assumption is that every set can be broken down into a sum of one-element sets. The absence of such a prohibition would lead to the derivation of a substantively absurd theorem stating that for every set, the value of the grey function is 0. However, in the case of an empty set, the application of the principle of additive convertibility would lead to a contradiction. Let us use an example to illustrate this problem.

Suppose we have a space $\Omega = \{1, 2, 3\}$. We can represent this set as the sum of one-element sets as follows: $\Omega = \{1\} \cup \{2\} \cup \{3\}$. Let us hypothetically assume the principle of additive convertibility for sets of one element. It would imply the following.

$$G^{\circ}(\Omega) = G^{\circ}(\{1\} \cup \{2\} \cup \{3\}) \Rightarrow G^{\circ}(\Omega) = G^{\circ}(\{1\}) + G^{\circ}(\{2\}) + G^{\circ}(\{3\}) \quad (1.2.1)$$

Given now Axiom 1 and Axiom 2, viz: $G^{\circ}(\Omega) = 1$ and $G^{\circ}(A_i) = 0 \Leftrightarrow A_i = a_i$, we obtain the following contradiction: $1 = 0+0+0$. Since the axioms cannot follow from or contradict each other, it is reasonable to introduce the prohibition of additive recalculability in the content of the last axiom.

The grey space concept allows for the theoretical unification of grey systems theory and, through it, different forms of grey information expression can be justified. Furthermore, thanks to the grey space concept, it is possible to introduce a demarcation criterion between methodological solutions that belong to grey systems theory and those whose belonging is questionable.

The basic element with which we can express grey information is grey numbers. They are a fundamental modelling tool in grey systems theory. The concept of grey space allows us to define a grey number in its most general sense, as in Definition 1.1.

Definition 1.1 If $\{\Omega, \mathcal{F}, G^{\circ}\}$, is a grey space and $\Omega \subset \mathcal{R}$ and A $\subset \mathcal{F}$, then the continuous grey number $\otimes$ is called an unknown number $d^* \in \mathcal{R}$, about which we can only say that: $\underline{a} \leq d^* \leq \overline{a}$, whereby: $\underline{a} = \inf(A), \overline{a} = \sup(A)$.

In many cases, grey systems theory does not use grey numbers, but other forms of grey information expression that can be derived from grey space. The form of grey information expression that is most commonly used in grey decision and evaluation models is the function of whiatenization. This is because the whitening function is a convenient tool for modelling the preferences and beliefs of experts or decision makers. Strictly speaking, this function is defined as in Definition 1.2.

Definition 1.2 Suppose we have a given grey space $\{\Omega, \mathcal{F}, G^{\circ}\}$ and the set $A \in \mathcal{F}$ and the set $Y = y \in R : 0 \leq y \leq 1$, then: $f : A \to Y$ is called a function of whiatenization when it satisfies the following conditions: $f(A) = 1$ when the set A is a one-element set and $f(\emptyset) = 0$.

The whitening function f differs from the grey function G° function in that the domain of the function f are the elements of the set $A \in \mathcal{F}$. This function captures the degree to which the subject of cognition believes that a given element is the preferred or desired one. In the case of the grey function, however G° the domain is not the elements of a set, but the sets themselves $A \in \mathcal{F}$. Consequently, the grey function reflects the level of uncertainty arising from the relationship of a given set $A \in \mathcal{F}$ in which the element of interest is certainly located, and the space of analysis Ω. The issue of grey functions in real-world applications does not play a role as much as whitening functions. Grey functions are important for the development of the theoretical foundations of GST and grey number algebraic systems. The main research efforts in this area are directed towards the search for analytical forms of greyness functions, which are traditionally called degree-of-greyness functions [28, 39, 40].

The theory of grey systems often uses methods in addition to grey numbers and whitening functions, which derive their theoretical status from the distributive interpretation of grey in data sets expressed in terms of white numbers. The distributive interpretation of greyscale is based on reasoning derived from the axiom of the prohibition of additivity of greyscale functions for one-element sets. The aforementioned reasoning can be presented in a structured form as follows ([25], pp. 206–207):

1. Suppose that we have a set of numbers representing some fragment of reality to us. It is important that these numbers are not grey numbers.
2. Since these numbers are not grey numbers, but are given as white numbers, relating this to grey space $\{\Omega, \mathcal{F}, G^{\circ}\}$, we can conclude that each such number is a one-element set belonging to F.
3. Since the numbers mentioned are one-element sets, the following axiom applies to them:

$$G^{\circ}(\cup_{i\in N} A_i) = \sum\nolimits_{i\in N} G^{\circ}(A_i), \text{ where}: \ A_i \cap A_j = \emptyset \wedge A_i \neq \{a_i\}$$

4. Analysing the axioms presented, the following interesting conclusion can be drawn: white numbers taken on their own have no greyness, or more formally: their greyness is zero. On the other hand, when we consider them as a whole set, such grayness does exist. In other words, there is a synergistic effect here that the sum of the qualities of the parts is not the same as the quality of the whole.
5. Hence, the conclusion is that even when the collected data are in the form of white numbers, as a whole they can still be of interest to grey systems theory because the grey function assigns values greater than and different from zero.

The reasoning presented here provides a theoretical basis for the analysis of data sequences organised as sets of white numbers. These sequences can be time series or sequences of data describing the state of some objects against an assumed set of criteria.

Data in the form of time series are important in grey predictive models. This type of sequence is also used in the study of relationships between features of a phenomenon using grey incidence analysis. On the other hand, data describing an object or set of objects against an adopted set of criteria are extremely important for grey decision-making and evaluation models.

However, no matter what type of data we want to analyse using models based on the distributive distribution of grey, the starting point of any analysis is the appropriate preprocessing of the data, involving the application of special mathematical operations called grey sequence opearators. The result of these transformations is to obtain a new sequence called a grey sequence. The entire computational process leading to the grey sequence is called generation of grey ([27], pp. 57–81, [32, 33], pp. 45–65).

The methodological justification of the preprocessing procedure using the generation of grey sequences enforces, at the epistemological level, the assumption of the deterministic nature of the phenomena analysed. It is assumed that, if the data are not random, they must always more or less reflect the mechanism governing the phenomenon in question. However, it often does not reveal itself in an obvious way in the collected data set, due to the complex network of factors influencing the phenomenon. In other words, the subject of cognition is hindered in the task of analysing and evaluating the mechanism in question in the research process. The research strategy that the subject of cognition therefore arbitrarily has to assume is: that the collected data contain information about the mechanism of interest in the phenomenon in question and are not random data, and that it is possible to eliminate or at least attenuate the information noise contained in the data through appropriate prepocessing procedures. In grey systems theory, these postulates are realised through the aforementioned process called generation of grey sequences.

1.3 Comparison of the Systems Approach in Grey Systems Theory and in Management Research

The systems paradigm is present today in many fields of scientific research and practical activity. The main ideas of this paradigm are, in principle, the same in different scientific disciplines, however, each of them creatively captures the issue in its own way. Adopting the classification proposed by Griffin [41], four basic approaches can be distinguished in management in a historical-logical perspective: classical, behavioural, quantitative, and integrative. In this classification, the system approach is embedded in the integrative approach. The integrative approach is the result of the intensive development of management science and the interpenetration of many methods, concepts, and ideas in the field.

Currently, we can divide the integrative approach into two approaches. The first is directly inspired by the ideas of Bertalanffy [42]. Treats the organisation as a system coupled to its environment, with its own internal structure, composed of subsystems that are interdependent. This view of organisations proposes holism, instead of the Cartesian view used by the classical management approach. It also points out that the optimisation of each part of an organisation individually does not necessarily lead to the optimisation of the whole, best exemplified by the 'bull whip' effect in supply chains [43]. In addition, this view pays attention to synergistic effects and the analysis of compression between system elements. Today, this approach has been further developed, as evidenced by the ideas proposed by Senge [44]. Their popularity among not only academics, but also managers, demonstrates that the systems paradigm continues to meet the needs of management theory and practice. The second approach in the integrative approach that draws on the system paradigm is the situational approach. It takes the concept of a system as a starting point, however, it focusses on the fact that any sociotechnical system is an extremely complex system. There are a multitude of compressions and dependencies between elements in it. By its very nature, a system of this type is a probabilistic system, and therefore the postulate that no two identical organisations can exist seems reasonable. The selection of management tools and models should therefore always take into account the specificity and environment of a particular organisation. The situational approach is distinguished by its great flexibility and lack of dogmatism, while paying attention to the environment in which the organisation operates. For this reason, it may still be attractive to modern managers.

Grey systems theory, as opposed to management, explicitly refers to a systems approach in its name. The question arises: is this just the result of a naming tradition, or does it have a deeper substantive justification? So far in the literature, the issue has been dealt with in two ways. The first is to use a figurative and intuitive take on the term grey system, without going into the meaningfulness of such nomenclature [23, 27, 45, 46]. The main focus here is on the cybernetic concept of a grey box. The second approach, on the other hand, is an attempt to frame the issue in the context of some philosophical and methodological tradition [25, 35]. Already at this point, it is possible to signal that in grey systems theory the systems approach has a very different meaning than in management science. In the latter it is pragmatic in nature, whereas in grey systems theory it is theoretical and cognitive in nature. In management sciences, the real organisation or process within it is to be analysed with the help of systems tools, whereas in grey systems theory, the system is only a convenient concept for methodological considerations. Briefly, these considerations can be summarised as follows: a system in grey systems theory is treated as something that exists objectively; however, the way it is known is subjective and dependent on the subject of cognition. This subjectivity makes it possible for the subject to produce information that is inadequate for the object being cognised. This effect in relation to a specific class of objects, such as systems, may manifest itself in that [25]:

- Information about the purpose of the system is not clear, which is caused by an error in the identification of the elements that make up the system; hence, we can speak of uncertainty in defining the boundaries of the system;
- The information about the elements of the system is inconsistent, which is due to the error that an element is not consistently assigned to the system and its sub-systems; we can therefore speak of uncertainty arising from contradictory information;
- Information about the system is redundant, which is caused by an error in the attribution of one element to several subsystems, so we can speak of uncertainty resulting from overlapping information;
- The information on subsystems or elements is not complete, resulting in an error where an essential element is not included in the description of the system; hence, we can speak of uncertainty resulting from incomplete information on the system;
- Information about the functions of the system is not unambiguous, with the result that the structure of the system is shaped in such a way that some functions are carried out redundantly by several subsystems, while others are completely ignored; we can therefore speak of uncertainty arising from the uncertainty of the structure of the system and the processes taking place within them.

Whether the systems approach in grey systems theory is based on the cybernetic concept of the black box or considerations embedded in a chosen methodological tradition, its main purpose is to investigate the nature of information and uncertainty. Investigating the nature of information is the specificity of the systems approach in grey systems theory, and it must be said that it is radically different in its aims and objectives than the systems approach practised in management science. This does not mean that grey systems theory models cannot be used in management research. On the contrary, their many properties related to the mastery of uncertain information are predisposed to the quantitative analysis of empirical data obtained from scientific research and practical activities in management.

Of course, one can look for other areas of research in management where the issue of uncertainty and information at such an advanced theoretical level may be useful. An example might be the problem of grey information and its relation to concepts such as knowledge or quality, but this will always be research whose usefulness in management practice and theory can be questioned. In summary, it can be said that grey systems theory uses, like management, a systems approach and also addresses the problem of uncertainty. However, it must be said that they are incompatible and incomparable.

1.4 Grey Systems Theory in Terms of Research Paradigms in Management Science

The concept of paradigm was introduced into the philosophy of science by Thomas Kuhn [47]. He did not define it explicitly, but it can be assumed that a paradigm is a certain set of binding assumptions adhered to by the community of scientists practising a particular discipline of science. This set of assumptions in the most general sense should refer to such issues as:

1. Criteria for the selection of scientific problems in a scientific field, i.e. what a scientific problem is and what a science does not consider to be a problem.
2. Issues related to ontological assumptions about the structure of the reality studied by a given science and assumptions about the possibilities and limits of scientific cognition.
3. Rules of scientific conduct, i.e. what are the recognised procedures and methods for conducting scientific research in a given discipline of knowledge.

The notion of paradigm therefore encompasses, on the one hand, issues of a theoretical nature and, on the other hand, issues of a cultural, sociological, or psychological nature associated with a particular group of scholars ([48], p. 47). Simplifying, one can say that it is a kind of research tradition in a given scientific field, where, as much as substantive issues, issues related to the values professed by scholars shape the development of knowledge in a given scientific discipline. This development of knowledge, according to Kuhn, does not proceed in a cumulative way, as Popper would have wished in his evolutionist conception of the development of science [49, 50]. On the contrary, such development takes place through scientific revolutions, which result in a paradigm shift to one that better explains the phenomena analysed in a given field of knowledge or that allows for the breaking of research stagnation in that field.

According to Kuhn, several stages of development in a field of knowledge can be distinguished. The first is the preparadigmatic period, where facts are collected in a haphazard manner, attempts are made to define the scope of a given field of knowledge, and competing ideas and concepts aspiring to become paradigms are formulated. We can call this period the preparadigmatic period. In the second period of development of a given field of knowledge, we can identify the dominant paradigm. A cumulative and systematic accumulation of knowledge then takes place. The next period is the stage in the development of a given field of knowledge where anomalies emerge that cause interpretative difficulties on the basis of the dominant paradigm. The accumulation of these anomalies leads to the scientific community of a given knowledge discipline beginning to engage in a discourse aimed at a paradigm shift. This takes place during the next period of development of a given field of knowledge, in which a new paradigm is formulated and the resulting scientific revolution begins to spread. At this stage, the old paradigm still finds many adherents; however, eventually there is a shift to a new way of thinking in a given science.

The concept of scientific revolution and the notion of paradigm have found an important place in the problems addressed by the philosophy of science. One of the more popular developments of this concept is the considerations proposed by Imre Lakatos [51, 52]. He did not use the concept of paradigm, but the term 'research programme'. The concept of research programmes is an attempt to reconcile Popper's falsificationism and Kuhn's concept of scientific revolution. Popper regarded science as the pursuit of truth. He ignored the history of science. He treated methodology as the ethics of the scientist. The making and falsifying of hypotheses was to serve the purpose of approaching the truth progressively. Hence, science in Popper's view has an evolutionary character characterised by the cumulative progress of knowledge. Kuhn, on the other hand, analysed the development of science in historical terms. He treated scientific research as a puzzle involving the matching of facts to the assumptions of an accepted paradigm. He assumed that for a variety of reasons, scientists do not immediately abandon their theories as soon as they encounter facts incompatible with them, as Popper postulated.

The research programme as a synthesis of these two approaches is a certain set of theories referring to one common idea. This common idea on which these theories are based is called the hard core of the research programme. In this sense, a research programme is something akin to a paradigm. However, the research programmeme assumes that hypotheses are put forward and falsified against the hard core. The methodology therefore, within the research programme itself, is normative. The problem, however, is that the hypotheses that are generated within a given research programme may be ad hoc hypotheses and therefore, according to Popper's assumptions, cannot be falsifiable. However, the concept of research programmes does not negate ad hoc hypotheses if they are hypotheses that protect the hard core of the research programme. If this protective belt of hypotheses allows the research programme to grow and be progressive, then making ad hoc hypotheses is a methodologically correct procedure. If, on the other hand, the research programme degenerates and the hard core protection belt does not provide progress in explaining the fragment of reality analysed in the discipline, then such a programme may be replaced by another, more creative, and progressive one. Interestingly, the concept of research programmes allows for a great deal of methodological pluralism, i.e. there can be many competing programmes that are progressive at any given time. This provides science with multiple perspectives on the phenomena or facts in question, which is the result of different references arising from the hard core of individual research programmes.

Against the backdrop of considering the issue of paradigms and research programmes, a fundamental question arises: can we identify and describe such paradigms and research programmes in the management sciences? The question is also this: Is it better to use the term paradigm or is it more appropriate to speak of research programmes in the management sciences? Taking only theoretical criteria and considering the current methodological state of the management sciences, it is better to use the term research programme ([53], p. 28). However, analysing the literature on the subject, it is worth noting that traditionally, when methodological issues are mentioned, the concept of paradigm usually appears and it is emphasised that management science is multi-paradigmatic [54–59]. There have been many attempts to classify these paradigms. It can be done in view of the separate subdisciplines of the management sciences or by identifying the main schools of management, understood as a set of scholars referring to a common epistemological basis in a given historical, geographical or cultural context. In addition, many authors attempt to classify paradigms by adopting various criteria that more or less attempt to embed management research methodologies in the context of the philosophy of science ([54], pp. 20–21).

However, assuming that management sciences are social sciences, it makes sense to distinguish paradigms in management research based on the very popular concept in the social sciences of Burell and Morgan [60]. This classification is based on two criteria. The first is a criterion related to the problem of cognition in which two states can be distinguished, i.e. objectivism and subjectivism. On the other hand, the second criterion is related to the sociology of regulation, in which the issues of regulation and change are distinguished. The problem of the sociology of regulation can be reduced to answering the question: What should be the main issue in research? Should the research concert on explaining social order and the pursuit of equilibrium, or should the research emphasis, however, be directed towards issues of conflict and change in social systems? ([55], p. 276).

With regard to the distinction between objective and subjective approaches, several issues that constitute such a division can be distinguished.

The first is to look at the issue of ontology in the social sciences. The subjective approach adopts nominalism, while the objective approach bases on realism. Nominalism treats general entities as products of human language and denies their objective existence. Realism, on the other hand, assumes that general entities exist independently of thought.

The second important issue is the perspective of epistemology in the social sciences. The subjective approach assumes antipositivism, while the objective approach assumes positivism. Anti-positivism assumes that in the social sciences it is impossible to study phenomena along the lines taken from the natural sciences because the beliefs, language and attitudes that the researcher adopts influence the results of the study. In this approach, the researcher is not a neutral observer, but an actor who influences the research process itself. Positivism, on the other hand, assumes the neutrality of the researcher and disregards his or her intuition and introspection. It argues that the social world, on the model of the physical world, is governed by laws that must be learnt empirically.

The third issue is the problematic view of human nature. The subjective approach assumes voluntarism and the objective approach assumes determinism. Voluntarism takes the free will of the individual as the most important force in social systems. Determinism rejects the concept of free will and assumes that a person's current behaviour and mental states are determined by past events.

The final issue that constitutes the division between objective and subjective approaches is the problem of methodology. The subjectivist approach assumes idiographic, while the objectivist approach assumes nomothetic. The idiographic approach in methodology presupposes in-depth individual research, while the nomothetic approach assumes that there are common features in a given group of studied phenomena or people, which can be studied in the context of the relations that occur between them and, on this basis, build scientific laws.

From the intersection of the two previously described criteria proposed for the classification of paradigms by Burell and Morgan, the following four paradigms were identified: radical structuralism, radical humanism, the interpretative paradigm, and the functionalist paradigm ([55], pp. 277–278). Modifications can be made to this typology to make it more relevant to management science issues. One such successful modification was made by Sułkowski [54]. He proposes a division in the management sciences into the following paradigms: neopositivist-functionalist-systemic (NFS), interpretivist-symbolic (IS), paradigm of radical structuralism or otherwise critical management studies (CMS), paradigm of radical humanism or otherwise postmodernism (POST).

Then the neo-positivist-functionalist-systems paradigm (NFS) assumes the causal nature of relationships in organisations. The aim is to study them objectively using quantitative methods. This paradigm assumes the concept of a fully rational human being. Research in this paradigm should be conducted by a neutral observer. The knowledge generated should be universal, verifiable, and intersubjectively communicable. The testability of this knowledge can be done on the grounds of falsificationism or verificationism. Therefore, the dominant approach to research methodology in this paradigm is the nomothetic approach.

The interpretivist-symbolic (IS) paradigm adopts the tenets of social constructivism, which assumes that during research the researcher cannot have the attitude of a neutral observer because people always perceive reality through the prism of their culture, upbringing, or experience, giving it an individual character and meaning. Therefore, in this paradigm, the boundary between practice and scientific cognition (particpation in action) is blurred. The dominant approach in terms of research methodology is the idiographic approach and the extensive use of qualitative methods in the research conducted.

The Critical Management Studies (CMS) paradigm emphasises the analysis of power relations and oppression in organisations. In this paradigm, the researcher is not axiologically neutral but, on the contrary, is committed to uncovering and stigmatising mechanisms of oppression. His role is to critique the existing organisational reality and attempt to change it. Therefore, this research paradigm is strongly ideologically entangled. The basic research methodology is based on the extensive use of qualitative methods.

The paradigm of radical humanism (POST) is characterised by a high level of inconsistency in its assumptions, intuitionism, criticism of and distrust of the scientific method. It is of marginal importance. In a sense, the approach in this paradigm can be considered unscientific and one has to agree with Sulkowski ([54], p. 23), that it is a kind of playfulness and intellectual provocation.

The four paradigms presented have influenced the development of management science to varying degrees. By far the dominant paradigm is the NFS paradigm, which attempts to construct research processes along the lines of the natural sciences. The use of a different paradigm always requires a deep methodological justification.

Analysing the state of research and the characteristics of grey systems theory, it can undoubtedly find application in research conducted in this paradigm. It can be, next to statistics, rough set theory or fuzzy logic, another way of analysing data. Furthermore, most of the research conducted in grey systems theory, as in the NFS paradigm, aims to fulfil the postulates of universality, testability, and intersubjective communicability. It should also be stated that the NFS paradigm interprets the nature of information and its uncertainty in the same way as grey systems theory. A particularly important point of commonality is the importance attributed to quantification procedures in mastering uncertainty. In addition to capturing grey in the context of the NFS paradigm, one can also look for the possibility of using the category of grey as a function of metaphor, which would be characteristic of other paradigms. This metaphoricity can inspire, evoke associations, introduce nonobvious lines of research and creative solutions. However, this is an area that has developed marginally. On the contrary, a logical and formal description of all concepts in grey systems theory is sought according to a methodological ideal such as that proposed in management in the NFS paradigm.

1.5 Grey Systems Theory and Research Strategies in Management Science

Given the complex research subject matter that management science deals with, a standard research procedure to increase the reliability and generalisability of results is triangulation. This methodological procedure starts with the assumption that every research method has limitations and drawbacks. Hence, to increase the credibility of the research conducted, results from different methods are compared [61]. This type of triangulation is called methodological triangulation. However, it can involve not only methods, but also other elements of the research process, such as data sources, researchers or theories ([62], pp. 247–249). Directly related to the problem of methodological triangulation is the problem of the appropriate design of the research process, which must take into account the following criteria [63]:

- The possibility of generalising the results to a specific population, which is related to the issue of external validity;
- Precision and control of the measurement of the behaviour of the variables under study, which is related to the problem of internal validity or construct validity;
- The realism of the context in which the research was conducted.

According to McGrath [61] simultaneous maximisation of these three criteria in the research process is impossible, which is called the 'three-horned dilemma.' Therefore, a logical consequence of such an assumption is that any research strategy must take into account the trade-off between the criteria mentioned.

Considering McGrath's concept of research method classification and their modification and development proposed by Scandura and Wiliams [63] we can distinguish and describe the following nine research strategies in the management sciences:

- Combination of formal theory and literature reviews—this is a research strategy to conceptualise a theoretical model, which will then be empirically tested; therefore, in this research strategy there is an interweaving of inductive and deductive thinking in the research process; the formal theory approach has a high level of generalisation, with a low level of contextual realism and precision and control in the measurement of variables; a very good example of this type of research in management science is the work of [64], in which, based on an analysis of the literature, the authors conceptualise the theoretical problematics of sustainable supply chains; another interesting example of the use of formal modelling is the work on the theoretical problematics of strategy [65] and work from the intersection of psychology and management science on the important business issue of proactivity [66].
- Sample survey is a research strategy to collect data on a population in such a way that it is possible to infer and generalise the results to the whole population on the basis of a sample from the population. In this strategy, the main effort is directed towards minimising the influence of context by selecting variables that are uncorrelated with it. This research strategy maximises the generalisability of the results with a low level of contextual realism and precision in the measurement and control of the research variables. This strategy is primarily based on the use of statistical analysis methods and is the primary research strategy in the evidence-based management approach [67].
- Laboratory experiment is a research strategy that, under specially prepared artificial conditions, is aimed at controlling the impact of variables on the studied phenomenon and thus eliminating errors that may affect the interpretation of the causal relations taking place; the experiment is often conducted in such a way that two research groups are selected: the first one is subjected to the experiment, while the second is a group serving as a control for the conducted research and is

not subjected to the experiment. Experimentation in the management sciences is not a dominant research strategy; however, in the literature there are several interesting research papers that usually deal with the issue of organisational behaviour analysis [68, 69] or issues related to public policy and management [70–72]. The laboratory experiment maximises the level of control of variables in the study; however, it exhibits low levels of generalisability of results and low contextual realism.

- Experimental simulation is a research strategy in which the researcher attempts to replicate realistically the context of the study through simulation scenarios of real-life situations. An interesting example of management research using experimental simulations is work addressing the issue of an organisation's openness to change [73], research analysing the impact of bureaucratic behaviour in the operation of public assistance agencies [74] and research analysing the impact of informal relationship networks in the context of organisational crisis [75]. Experimental simulations are characterised by an average high level of precision in the measurement of variables and an average high level of contextual realism, while in terms of the level of generalisability of the results, this should be considered low.
- Field study that used primary data is a research strategy that aims to analyse behaviour in a real-world context; a characteristic feature of this type of field research is the frequent methodological integration and interweaving of qualitative and quantitative approaches [76–82]. This research strategy maximises the realism of the context while providing a low level of control for the variables under study, and this strategy also in the absence of a representative sample can lead to a low level of generalisation of results.
- Field study that used secondary data is a research strategy that uses data not collected by the researcher. A classic example of this type of approach is research that aggregates the results of studies available from different sources of information and, on this basis, performs a meta-analysis that verifies specific research hypotheses. An example of the application of this type of strategy in management research can be found in the work of Stringer [83] in the field of finance or in the work on hotel management research [84].
- Field experiment is a research strategy that aims to conduct an experiment in real rather than artificial or laboratory conditions; this type of research strategy is characterised by a medium–high level of measurement control of the variables under study and a medium–high level of contextual realism, with a low level of generalisation of the results obtained. The field experiment in the social sciences has lived to see many methodological studies [85–88]. Examples of its application in management science include work on risk management [89], work on motivation monitoring research [90] or work on knowledge management issues [91].
- Expert research (judgment tasks)—is a research strategy that uses expert knowledge to assess the relationships under investigation. Usually experts are participants in the process being studied. This type of research strategy is characterised by a medium–high level of generalisation of results and a medium–high level of control of the measurement of the variables under study, while maintaining a low

level of realism of the research context. Citing Scandura and Williams [63], an example of the application of this type of research in management science can be found in the work of analysing exit barriers in the context of strategic management issues [92].

- Computer simulation is a research strategy that involves the creation of artificial data to represent the functioning of a real-world object of analysis using computer-based techniques. This type of strategy has a medium–high level of generalisability of results and a medium–high level of contextual realism, with a low level of control over the measurement of variables in the study. Computer simulations in management and quality sciences with the development of information technology and intelligent computing methods are increasingly used; the extent of their application can be thoroughly penetrated in many detailed and domain-orientated systematic literature reviews [93–95].

The literature highlights many advantages of triangulation, in particular the holistic and broad view of the research problem and the rationale for integrating or verifying often competing ways of thinking about the phenomenon under study. Furthermore, the triangulation procedure can inspire the creation of new methodological solutions and popularise interdisciplinarity in research. The disadvantages of the triangulation procedure undoubtedly include the difficulty in replicating research and the often biased selection of research methods and strategies resulting from the researcher's personal preferences. Furthermore, methodological triangulation in a conservative methodological approach may come across as a form of methodological eclecticism, whose epistemological status may be questionable. However, despite these objections, triangulation is a methodological concept that should be considered useful in management sciences. These sciences are interdisciplinary and multiparadigmatic in nature, and consequently, the set of methods acceptable for research is numerous. Hence, the design of research processes based on different research strategies and methods to increase the reliability of the results obtained seems logically justified.

The applicability of grey systems theory follows directly from the characteristics of the theoretical constructs used in the theory. They imply the structure of the data required to model specific scientific and practical problems. Table 1.1 brings together a description and characterisation of grey systems theory in this respect, while making a comparison with other approaches to uncertainty modelling, i.e. fuzzy logic and probabilistic approaches. Such a comparison aims to show the broader context of grey systems theory against the background of uncertainty modelling theories with a longer and more established tradition in management science. This comparison was made on the basis of the literature on the subject and, in particular, building on the proposal of Liu and Lin [27], which has been modified and integrated in terms of an axiomatic account of grey based on grey space. The original modification of this comparison in such terms was proposed by Mierzwiak and Nowak [96].

Table 1.1 Characteristics of grey systems theory with other approaches to uncertainty modelling

Comparative criteria	Grey systems theory	Fuzzy logic	Probabilistics
The underlying theoretical construct	Grey space	Fuzzy set	Probabilistic space
The basic function is determined on the underlying theoretical construct	Grey function	Set membership function	Probability density function
Number of data required	There may be little data	There may be little data	There must be a lot of data
Nature of the data	They may be imprecise and incomplete expressed by grey numbers, whitening functions, or in distributive terms	They may be imprecise and incomplete expressed in natural language	They must be precise, expressed through quantitative data series

Analysing the summary in Table 1.1, we can conclude that the grey function and the grey space are theoretical constructs that clearly distinguish grey systems theories from probabilistic or fuzzy approaches. On the other hand, as for the number of data needed for the analysis, it is often emphasised that this is the domain of grey systems theory. However, we must be aware that fuzzy logic has very similar properties but differs from grey systems theory in that it prefers data with different characteristics. The probabilistic approach, on the other hand, is based on large and precisely defined data sets. In this type of data, it should be the preferred analytical methodology. Substituting fuzzy logic or grey system theory should be considered a methodological error in the construction of the research process.

Considering the methodological characteristics of grey systems theory and the research strategies in management science proposed by Scandura and Wiliams [63], Table 1.2 identifies the application potential of grey systems theory in management science research.

When analysing the application potential of grey systems theory, it is worth signalling the problem of generalisation of the results obtained ([36], p. 75, [97], pp. 109–110). Because the mathematical properties of grey analytical methods allow work on sparse data, it is often wrongly assumed that this property is the same as the ability to generalise the results. The level of generalisation of the results will always depend on the quality of the empirical base collected. On the other hand, the methodology of data analysis will be important in terms of what these data are structured, as well as how and in what form they are expressed.

Table 1.2 Application potential of grey systems theory in management research strategies

Research strategy	Description of the potential for application of the grey system theory
Combination of formal theory and literature review approaches	In this strategy, the application potential of grey systems theory is negligible. The grey system can only be useful as a metaphor to describe an organisation. In the context of literature analysis, on the other hand, an approach based on descriptive statistics and statistical methods for classifying collected studies on the basis of keywords or the content of abstracts is by far the most preferred analytical methodology. Often in literature analysis, expert knowledge is used in the selection or evaluation of research material, which may give room for a wider application of grey analytical methods as a sub-method in the research strategy under analysis
Sample surveys	In this research strategy, the application potential of grey systems theory is low, as the empirical material collected should be characterised by precision and representativeness with respect to the population under study. Therefore, this is definitely a research area where a statistical approach is used. In this research, it is possible to use grey systems theory when collecting precise data is difficult or expensive. In such a case, one can opt for approximate data expressed by grey numbers and use them in analytical statistical models. The grey numbers in such hybrid models are far more successful in terms of ease of calculation and interpretation than the fuzzy numbers, which are possible in this case but difficult and inconvenient. Therefore, they have data expressed by linguistic features without much loss in analysis. It may be expedient to transform them into grey numbers
Laboratory experiment	In this research strategy, grey systems theory is not applicable. In a formal sense, it is possible to apply grey analytical techniques; however, this would contradict the idea of the laboratory experiment itself, where the essential aim is to maintain the maximum precision of the variables under study and to control them fully in the research process
Experimental simulations	In this research strategy, the application potential of grey systems theory is low, because in experimental simulations, as in a laboratory experiment, an important element is the control of the variables under study. However, experimental simulations strive to reproduce the realism of the context, which may give room for the application of grey systems theory, since, in order to obtain realistic simulation scenarios, a precise and accurate description of the variables is not always expedient or advisable

(continued)

Table 1.2 (continued)

Research strategy	Description of the potential for application of the grey system theory
Field study that used primary data	In this research strategy, the application potential of grey systems theory is medium, because this strategy, in its specificity, implies the interweaving of quantitative and qualitative approaches. Consequently, in these studies, often the variables are not precise and are underdetermined. In addition, there is a tendency in this type of research to obtain as real a study context as possible, at the expense of multiplicity and representativeness of the sample, which may favour grey and fuzzy analytical methods in the development of results
Field study that used secondary data	In this research strategy, the application potential of grey systems theory is low, because this strategy implies the integration of research results from multiple sources, and the data are not directly collected by the researcher. Data integration can be done qualitatively or quantitatively. In the case of a qualitative approach, the grey system theory can only be applied in the selection or evaluation of research material using expert knowledge. In the case of a quantitative approach, on the other hand, integration is done through meta-analysis, which uses advanced statistical inference for secondary knowledge discovery. It is worth noting that this approach to the collected research material makes this research strategy similar to a systematic literature review. In such a case, grey systems theory is of little use
Field experiment	In this research strategy, the application potential of grey systems theory is medium. This is due to the fact that in a train experiment, the level of control of the variables under study is not as restrictive as in artificial laboratory conditions. Hence, the data obtained may be imprecise and incomplete. Furthermore, the number of data may be insufficient for statistical analysis due to the unitary nature of the research process. Under such conditions, grey analytical methods can be considered as much as possible in the development of research results

(continued)

Table 1.2 (continued)

Research strategy	Description of the potential for application of the grey system theory
Expert research (judgment tasks)	In this research strategy, the application potential of grey systems theory is high. This is because, in modelling expert knowledge, grey theoretical constructs such as whitening functions or grey numbers can be highly useful in quantitatively modelling imprecise linguistic judgements made by experts. These judgements owe their imprecision and underdetermination to the fact that they are based not only on rationality, but also on intuition. It is also worth adding that grey methods integrate very easily with approaches such as fuzzy cognitive maps, network thinking, or other methods with origins in systems theory and engineering, in which the starting point is the mathematical representation of knowledge of a qualitative and quantitative nature
Computer simulation	In this research strategy, the application potential of grey systems theory is high. This is because the simulation models that are built can increase the quality of the representation of the complex reality of management processes by modelling data that are approximate and imprecise in nature. The source of this uncertainty in the data is the human activity in any management process, which is very difficult to describe mathematically at the level of nontrivial managerial issues

References

1. Harrison, E.F.: Interdisciplinary models of decision making. Manag. Decis. **31** (1993).
2. Harrison, E.F., Pelletier, M.A.: The essence of management decision. Manag. Decis. **38**(9), 462–470 (2000)
3. Islam, S.: Evaluation of low-carbon sustainable technologies in agriculture sector through grey ordinal priority approach. Int. J. Grey Syst. **1**(7), 5–26 (2021)
4. Kotarbinski, T.: Elements of the Theory of Knowledge, Formal Logic and Methodology of Science (in Polish). PWN, Warsaw (1966)
5. Mantura, W.: Overview of Qualitology. Publishing House of Poznan University of Technology, Poznań (2021)
6. Ostasiewicz, W.: Quantification of Social Features. Research Papers of Wrocław University of Economics, pp. 167–173 (2006)
7. Stevens, S.S.: On the theory of scales of measurement. Science **103**(6), 677–680 (1946)
8. Lobanov, A.S.: The basic concepts of qualimetry. Scientific and Technical Information Processing **40**(4), 72–82 (2013)
9. Azgaldov, G., Kostin, A., Omiste, Á.P.: The ABC of Qualimetry. LAP LAMBERT Academic Publishing, Ridero (2018)
10. Azgaldov, G.G., Kostin, A.V.: Applied qualimetry: its origins, errors and misconceptions. Benchmarking Int. J. **18**(5), 428–444 (2011)
11. Borys, T.: Category of Quality and Statistical Comparative analysis (in Polish). Publishing house of Wroclaw University of Economics and Business, Wrocałw (1984)
12. Kolman, R.: Qualitology-science of quality (in Polsh). Mechanik **44**, 457 (1971)
13. Kolmogorov, A.N.: Foundations of the theory of probability. Martino Fine Books, New York (2013)
14. Jaynes, E.T.: Probability Theory. Cambridge University Press (2003)

15. Cox, R.T.: Probability, frequency and reasonable expectation. Am. J. Phys. **14**(1), 1–13 (1946)
16. Cox, R.T.: Algebra of probable inference. Johns Hopkins University Press (2001)
17. Jeffreys, H.: Scientific Inference, 3rd edn. Cambridge University Press, Cambridge (1974)
18. Zadeh, L.A.: Fuzzy sets. Inf. Control **8**, 338–353 (1965)
19. Young, R.C.: The algebra of many-valued quantities. Math. Ann. **104**(12), 260–290 (1931)
20. Deng, J.: Control problems of grey systems. Syst. Control. Lett. **1**(3), 288–294 (1982)
21. Deng, J.: Grey Control System. Printing House of Central China University of Science and Technology, Hubei (1985)
22. Delcea, C.: Grey systems theory in economics-a historical applications review. Grey Syst. Theory Appl. **5**, 263–276 (2015)
23. Delcea, C.: Not black not even white definitively grey economic systems. J. Grey Syst. **26**, 11–26 (2014)
24. Deng, J.: Introduction to grey system theory. J. Grey Syst. **1**, 1–24 (1989)
25. Mierzwiak, R., Xie, N., Nowak, M.: A new axiomatic approach to the concept of grey information. Grey Syst. Theory Appl. **8**, 199–209 (2018)
26. Li, G.-D., Yamaguchi, D., Nagai, M.: A grey-based decision-making approach to the supplier selection problem. Math. Comput. Model. **46**, 573–581 (2007)
27. Liu, S., Lin, Y.: Grey Information: Theory and Practical Applications. Springer Science and Business Media (2006)
28. Liu, S., Fang, Z., Forrest, J.: On algorithm rules of interval grey numbers based on the "Kernel" and the degree of greyness of grey numbers. In: IEEE International Conference on Systems, Man and Cybernetics, Istanbul, IEEE, pp. 756–760 (2010)
29. Liu, S., Fang, Z., Yang, Y., Forrest, J.: General grey numbers and their operations. Grey Syst. Theory Appl. **2**, 341–349 (2012)
30. Xie, N.: On computational algorithms of grey numbers based on information background. Grey Syst.: Theory Appl. **3**, 177–190 (2013)
31. Xie, N., Pearman, A.D.: Comparing grey number weights under interval probability information background. J. Grey Syst. **27**, 21–38 (2015)
32. Liu, S., Yang, Y., Forrest, J.: Grey Data Analysis. Springer, Berlin (2017)
33. Liu, S., Zhang, H. and Yang, Y.: Explanation of terms of grey incidence analysis models. Grey Syst. Theory Appl. (2017)
34. Javanmardi, E., Liu, S.: Exploring the human cognitive capacity in understanding systems: a grey systems theory perspective. Found. Sci. **7** (2019)
35. Javanmardi, E., Liu, S., Xie, N.: Exploring the philosophical paradigm of grey systems theory as a postmodern theory. Found. Sci. **11** (2019)
36. Mierzwiak, R.: Characteristics of selected approaches of uncertainty modelling in the context of management sciences. Publishing House of Rzeszow University of Technology, p. 67 (2019)
37. Nowak, M., Borowiec, A.: Intuitive solution of decision-making problems using the grey systems theory. Organ. Rev. 28–35 (2019)
38. Xie, N.: Explanations about grey information and framework of grey system modeling. Grey Syst. Theory Appl. **7**(8), 179–193 (2017)
39. Mierzwiak, R., Nowak, M., Xie, N.: A new approach to the degree of greyness. Grey Syst. Theory Appl. **11**(2), 241–252 (2021)
40. Liu, S., Lin, Y.: A new deflnition on degree of greyness of grey numbers with several theorems. Tuscon IEEE Netw. Sens. Control. (2005)
41. Griffin, R.W.: Management. 11th edn. Cengage Learning, Hampshire (2012)
42. Von Bertalanffy, L.: Organismic Psychology and Systems Theory. Clark University Press (1968)
43. Lee, H.L., Padmanabhan, V., Whang, S.: The bullwhip effect in supply chains. Sloan Manag. Rev. **38**, 93–102 (1997)
44. Senge, P.M.: The Fifth Discipline: The Art and Practice of the Learning Organization. Broadway Business (2006)
45. Andrew, A.M.:, Why the world is grey? Grey Syst. Theory Appl. **1**(8), 112–116 (2011)

46. Li, Q., Lin, Y.: Review paper: a briefing to grey systems theory. J. Syst. Sci. Inf. **2**(4), 178–192 (2014)
47. Kuhn, T.S.: The Structure of Scientific Revolutions. University of Chicago Press, Chicago (1962)
48. Orman, T.F.: Paradigm as a central concept in Thomas Kuhn's thought. Int. J. Humanit. Soc. Sci. **6**, 47–52 (2016)
49. Popper, K.R.: The Logic of Scientific Discovery. Conhecimento Ob/etivo (1972a)
50. Popper, K.R.: Objective Knowledge: An Evolutionary Approach. Oxford University Press (1972b)
51. Lakatos, I.: Criticism and the methodology of scientific research programmes. Proceedings of the Aristotelian Society, pp. 149–186. Oxford University Press, London (1968)
52. Lakatos, I.: Falsification and the methodology of scientific research programmes. In: Harding, S. (ed.) Can Theories Be Refuted?, pp. 205–259. Springer, Dordrecht (1976)
53. Gospodarek, T.: Representative management as a rational research program in Kuhn-Lakatos-Laudan sense. Int. J. Econ. Bus. Res. **1**, 409–421 (2009)
54. Sulkowski, Ł.: The paradigms of management sciences. Contemp. Manag. Q. **12** (2013)
55. Hassard, J.: Multiple paradigms and organizational analysis: a case study. Organ. Stud. **12**, 275–299 (1991)
56. Lertzman, K.: The paradigm of management, management systems, and resource stewardship. J. Ethnobiol. **29**, 339–358 (2009)
57. Sułkowski, Ł.: Theories, paradigms, metaphors and ideologies of management - different ways of performing organizational and managerial discourse. Research Papers of Wrocław University of Economics, pp. 131–143. (2016)
58. Mathieu, J.E., Chen, G.: The etiology of the multilevel paradigm in management research. J. Manag. **37**, 610–641 (2011)
59. Modell, S.: Bridging the paradigm divide in management accounting research: the role of mixed methods approaches. Manag. Account. Res. **21**, 124–129 (2010)
60. Burrell, G., Morgan, G.: Sociological Paradigms and Organizational Analysis. Heinemann London (1979)
61. McGrath, J.E.: Dilemmatics. The study of research choices and dilemmas. Am. Behav. Sci. **25**(11), 179–210 (1981)
62. Stańczyk, S.: Fundamentals of research methodology in management sciences (in Polish). In: Czakon, W. (ed.), pp. 247–249. Wolters Kluwer Business (2015)
63. Scandura, T.A., Williams, E.A.: Research methodology in management: current practices, trends, and implications for future research. Acad. Manag. J. **43**(12), 1248–1264 (2000)
64. Seuring, S., Müller, M.: From a literature review to a conceptual framework for sustainable supply chain management. J. Clean. Prod. **16**(10), 1699–1710 (2008)
65. Steen, E.V.: A formal theory of strategy. Manag. Sci. **63**(8), 2616–2636 (2017)
66. Lieder, F., Iwama, G.: Toward a formal theory of proactivity. Cogn. Affect. Behav. Neurosci. **21**(3), 490–508 (2021)
67. Rousseau, D.M. (ed.): The Oxford Handbook of Evidence-Based Management. Oxford University Press (2012)
68. Katok, E.: Using laboratory experiments to build better operations management models. Found. Trends® Technol. Inf. Oper. Manag. **5**, 1–86 (2011)
69. Siemen, E.: The usefulness of behavioral laboratory experiments in supply chain management research. J. Supply Chain. Manag. **47**(7), 17–18
70. Bozeman, B.: Experimental design in public policy and management research: an introduction. J. Public Adm. Res. Theory 10 (1992)
71. Bozeman, B., Scott, P.: Laboratory experiments in public policy and management. J. Public Adm. Res. Theory **7** (1992)
72. Cummings, R.G., Holt, C.A., Laury, S.K.: Using laboratory experiments for policymaking: an example from the Georgia irrigation reduction auction. J. Policy Anal. Manage. **23**, 341–363 (2004)

73. Devos, G., Buelens, M., Bouckenooghe, D.: Contribution of content, context, and process to understanding openness to organizational change: two experimental simulation studies. J. Soc. Psychol. **147**(12), 607–630 (2007)
74. Scott, P.G., Pandey, S.K.: The influence of red tape on bureaucratic behaviour: an experimental simulation. J. Policy Anal. Manage. **19**, 615–633 (2000)
75. Krackhardt, D., Stern, R.N.: Informal networks and organizational crises: an experimental simulation. Soc. Psychol. Q. **51**(6), 123 (1988)
76. Doolen, T.L., et al.: Kaizen events and organizational performance: a field study. Int. J. Prod. Perform. Manag. **57**(10), 637–658 (2008)
77. Khan, E.A., Quaddus, M.: Examining the influence of business environment on socio-economic performance of informal microenterprises. Int. J. Sociol. Soc. Policy **35**(4), 273–288 (2015)
78. Nuruzzaman, M.: Improving competitiveness in manufacturing-wholesaling-retailing supply chains. In: Advances in Business Marketing and Purchasing, pp. 221–457. Emerald Group Publishing Limited (2015)
79. Rahman, A.: Toward a comprehensive conceptualization of digital divide and its impact on e-government system success. In: Advances in Business Marketing and Purchasing, pp. 291–488. Emerald Group Publishing Limited (2015)
80. Urumsah, D.: Factors influencing consumers to use e-services in indonesian airline companies. In: E-services Adoption: Processes by Firms in Developing Nations, pp. 5–254. Emerald Group Publishing Limited (2015)
81. Sridharan, V.G.: Methodological insights theory development in qualitative management control: revisiting the roles of triangulation and generalization. Account. Audit. Account. J. 34(12), 451–479 (2020)
82. Zhang, R., Wang, J., Hao, J.-X.: how does knowledge heterogeneity affect transactive memory system in innovation? Evidence from a field study. J. Knowl. Manag. **24**(7), 1965–1985 (2020)
83. Stringer, C.: Empirical performance management research: observations fromAOSandMAR. Qual. Res. Account. Manag. **4**(6), 92–114 (2007)
84. Baloglu, S., Assante, L.M.: A content analysis of subject areas and research methods used in five hospitality management journals. J. Hosp. Tour. Res. **23**(2), 53–70 (1999)
85. Armantier, O., Boly, A.: On the external validity of laboratory experiments on corruption. In: Serra, D., Wantchekon, L. (eds.) Research in Experimental Economics, pp. 117–144. Emerald Group Publishing Limited, Bingley (2012)
86. Cardenas, J.C., Carpenter, J.P.: Three themes on field experiments and economic development. In: Harrison, G.W., Carpenter, J., List, J.A. (eds.) Research in Experimental Economics, pp. 71–123. Emerald (MCB UP), Bingley (2005)
87. Carpenter, J.P., Harrison, G.W., List, J.A.: Field experiments in economics: an introduction. In: Research in Experimental Economics, pp. 1–15. Bingley, Emerald (MCB UP) (2005)
88. Kraus, S., Meier, F., Niemand, T.: Experimental methods in entrepreneurship research: the status quo. Int. J. Entrep. Behav. Res. **22**(9), 958–983 (2016)
89. Cole, S., Giné, X. and Vickery, J.: How Does Risk Management Influence Production Decisions? Evidence from a Field Experiment. Rev. Financ. Stud. **30**(3), 1935–1970 (2017)
90. Nagin, D.S., Rebitzer, J.B., Sanders, S., Taylor, L.J.: Monitoring, motivation, and management: the determinants of opportunistic behavior in a field experiment. Am. Econ. Rev. **92**(8), 850–873 (2002)
91. Wang, S., Noe, R.A., Wang, Z.-M.: Motivating knowledge sharing in knowledge management systems. J. Manag. **40**(7), 978–1009 (2011)
92. Harrigan, K.R.: Exit barriers and vertical integration. Acad. Manag. J. **28**(9), 686–697 (1985)
93. Negahban, A., Smith, J.S.: Simulation for manufacturing system design and operation: Literature review and analysis. J. Manuf. Syst. **33**(4), 241–261 (2014)
94. Shou, W., Wang, J., Wu, P.: The application of simulation in lean production research: a critical review and future directions. Eng. Constr. Arch. Manag. 5 (2021). Volume ahead-of-print
95. Yoon, M., Bekker, J.: Multi-objective simulation optimisation on discrete sets: a literature review. Int. J. Oper. Res. **39**, 364 (2020)

96. Mierzwiak, R., Nowak, M.: Decision-Making Models in Grey Systems Theory (in Polish). PTE Poznań, Poznań (2020)
97. Mierzwiak, R., Xie, N., Dong, W. (2019). Classification of research problems in grey system theory based on grey space concept. J. Grey Syst. **31**

Chapter 2
Characteristics of Grey Analytic Models and Their Application Potential in Management Science Research

2.1 Grey Numbers in Modelling Management Problems

There are many proposals in the literature for the classification of grey numbers. Basically, we can divide these numbers according to two classification criteria. The first distinguishes discrete and continuous numbers. On the other hand, the second criterion divides the grey numbers into finite and infinite grey numbers. In order to formally describe the properties of the different types of numbers, let us adopt the following set of designations.

- $\otimes = d^* \in [\underline{a}, \overline{a}]$ - designation for continuous grey numbers,
- $\otimes = d^* \in a_1, \ldots, a_i, \ldots a_n$ - designation for discrete grey numbers.

  where:

- $\underline{a}$ - denotes the lower limit of the interval in which the grey number is located. The lower limit is also the smallest element of set A, hence it is also possible to denote $minA$,
- $\overline{a}$ - denotes the upper limit of the interval in which the grey number is located. The upper limit is also the largest element of the set A, so it is also possible to denote $maxA$,
- at the same time, it is assumed that the condition must be met that $\overline{a}$ $(maxA) \geq \underline{a}$ $(minA)$
- a_i denotes the *i-th* element of the set *A*,
- At the same time, it is assumed that the condition that the $a_{k-1} \leq a_k \leq a_{k+1}$

Taking into account the designations presented and the classification criteria, a distinction can be made in the set of finite numbers:

The original version of the chapter has been revised. A correction to this chapter can be found at https://doi.org/10.1007/978-981-97-2413-0_5

R. Mierzwiak, *Methodological Aspects of Grey Systems Theory in Management Research*, Series on Grey System, https://doi.org/10.1007/978-981-97-2413-0_2

- continuous white numbers:

$$d^* \in [\underline{a}, \overline{a}] \wedge (\underline{a} = \overline{a})$$

Example: [1;1], [10;10], [0,1;0,1]

- discrete white numbers:

$$d^* \in a_1, \ldots, a_i, \ldots a_n \wedge (n = 1)$$

example: {1;1},{10;10},{0,1;0,1}

- finite grey numbers of discrete nature, i.e. those which must satisfy the following condition:

$$|A| \neq \infty \wedge (\min A \neq \max A) \wedge (\min A \wedge \max A) \neq \infty$$

example: {1,2,3};{4,5,6};{0,1;0,2;0,3}
In contrast, in a set of finite grey numbers, we can identify:

- compartmentalised black numbers:

$$d^* \in [\underline{a}, \overline{a}] \wedge (\underline{a} = -\infty) \wedge (\overline{a} = +\infty)$$

example: [–∞; + ∞]

- discrete black numbers:

$$d^* \in a_1, \ldots, a_i, \ldots a_n \wedge (a_1 = -\infty) \wedge (n = +\infty)$$

example: {–∞,…, + ∞}

- discrete infinite grey numbers with a lower bound:

$$d^* \in a_1, \ldots, a_i, \ldots a_n \wedge (a_1 \neq \infty) \wedge (n = +\infty)$$

example: {–1;0;1…. +∞} {2;3…. +∞} {0,1;0,2;0,3… +∞}

- continuous infinite grey numbers with a lower limit:

$$d^* \in [\underline{a}, \overline{a}] \wedge (\underline{a} \neq -\infty) \wedge (\overline{a} = +\infty)$$

example: [–1; +∞]; [2; +∞]; [0,1; +∞]

- discrete infinite grey numbers with an upper limit:

$$d^* \in a_1, \ldots, a_i, \ldots a_n \wedge (a_1 = -\infty) \wedge (n \neq +\infty)$$

example: {−∞. ..-1; 0;1}; {−∞. ..1;2;3};{−∞. ..0,1; 0,2;0,3}

- continuous infinite grey numbers with an upper limit:

$$d^* \in \left[\underline{a}, \overline{a}\right] \wedge \left(\underline{a} = -\infty\right) \wedge (\overline{a} \neq +\infty)$$

example: [−∞; 1]; [−∞; 3] [−∞; 0, 3]

- continuous infinite grey numbers with lower and upper limits, which for simplicity are called interval grey numbers; these are grey numbers satisfying the following condition:

$$(|A| = \infty) \wedge [(\min A \wedge \max A) \neq \infty]$$

example: [–1;1],[1,2], [0,1;0,2]

From the point of view of practical applications, the most important type of grey numbers and the most commonly used are the interval grey numbers. The rules for operations on them can be reduced to a set of rules as follows [1, 2, 3]:

Rule 1: Suppose that $\otimes_1 \in \left[\underline{a_1}, \overline{a_1}\right], \underline{a_1}, < \overline{a_1}, \otimes_2 \in \left[\underline{a_2}, \overline{a_2}\right], \underline{a_2}, < \overline{a_2}$, is the sum of $\otimes_1$ and $\otimes_2$ is:

$$\otimes_1 + \otimes_2 \in \left[\underline{a_1} + \underline{a_2}, \overline{a_2} + \overline{a_2}\right]$$

Example: $\otimes_1 \in [1, 2]$, $\otimes_2 \in [3, 4]$, $\otimes_1 + \otimes_2 \in [4, 6]$

Rule 2: Suppose $\otimes_1 \in \left[\underline{a_1}, \overline{a_1}\right], \underline{a_1}, < \overline{a_1}, \otimes_2 \in \left[\underline{a_2}, \overline{a_2}\right], \underline{a_2}, < \overline{a_2}$, is the difference $\otimes_1$ and $\otimes_2$ is:

$$\otimes_1 - \otimes_2 \in \left[\underline{a_1} - \overline{a_2}, \overline{a_1} - \underline{a_2}\right]$$

Example: $\otimes_1 \in [1, 2]$, $\otimes_2 \in [3, 4]$, $\otimes_1 - \otimes_2 \in [-3, -1]$

Rule 3: Suppose $\otimes_1 \in \left[\underline{a_1}, \overline{a_1}\right], \underline{a_1}, < \overline{a_1}, \otimes_2 \in \left[\underline{a_2}, \overline{a_2}\right], \underline{a_2}, < \overline{a_2}$, is the product of $\otimes_1$ and $\otimes_2$ is:

$$\otimes_1 \cdot \otimes_2 \in \left[min\left(\underline{a_1} \cdot \underline{a_2}, \underline{a_1} \cdot \overline{a_2}, \overline{a_1} \cdot \underline{a_2}, \overline{a_1} \cdot \overline{a_2}\right), \max\left(\underline{a_1} \cdot \underline{a_2}, \underline{a_1} \cdot \overline{a_2}, \overline{a_1} \cdot \underline{a_2}, \overline{a_1} \cdot \overline{a_2}\right)\right]$$

Example: $\otimes_1 \in [1, 2]$, $\otimes_2 \in [3, 4]$, $\otimes_1 \cdot \otimes_2 \in [3, 8]$

Rule 4: Suppose $\otimes_1 \in \left[\underline{a_1}, \overline{a_1}\right], \underline{a_1}, < \overline{a_1}, \otimes_2 \in \left[\underline{a_2}, \overline{a_2}\right], \underline{a_2}, < \overline{a_2}$, is the quotient of $\otimes_1$ and $\otimes_2$ is:

$$\otimes_1/\otimes_2 \in \left[min\left(\underline{a_1}/\underline{a_2}, \underline{a_1}/\overline{a_2}, \overline{a_1}/\underline{a_2}, \underline{\overline{a_1}}/\overline{a_2}\right), max\left(\underline{a_1}/\underline{a_2}, \underline{a_1}/\overline{a_2}, \underline{\overline{a_1}}/\underline{a_2}, \overline{a_1}/\overline{a_2}\right)\right]$$

Example: $\otimes_1 \in [3, 4], \otimes_2 \in [5, 10], \otimes_1/\otimes_2 \in [0.3, 0.8]$

Rule 5: Suppose $\otimes \in \left[\underline{a}, \overline{a}\right], \underline{a}, < \overline{a}$, then the additive inversion operation is given as follows:

$$-\otimes \in \left[-\overline{a}, -\underline{a},\right]$$

Example: $\otimes \in [1, 2], -\otimes \in [-2, -1]$

Rule 6: Suppose $\otimes \in \left[\underline{a}, \overline{a}\right], \underline{a}, < \overline{a}, \underline{a} \neq 0, \ \overline{a} \neq 0, \ \underline{a} \cdot \overline{a} > 0$ then the operation of the inverse of $\otimes$ is given as:

$$\otimes^{-1} \in \left[\frac{1}{\overline{a}}, \frac{1}{\underline{a}}\right]$$

Example: $\otimes \in= [2, 4] \ \otimes^{-1} = [0.25, 0, 5]$

Rule 7: Suppose $\otimes \in \left[\underline{a}, \overline{a}\right], \ \underline{a}, < \overline{a}$, then the scalar multiplication operation is given as follows:

$$\mathrm{k} \cdot \otimes \in \left[\mathrm{k} \cdot \underline{a}, \mathrm{k} \cdot \overline{a}\right]$$

Example: $\otimes \in [2, 4], \mathrm{k} = 5, \mathrm{k} \cdot \otimes = 5 \cdot [2, 4] = [10, 20]$

Rule 8: Suppose that $\otimes \in \left[\underline{a}, \overline{a}\right], \ \underline{a}, < \overline{a}$, then the triplication operation is given as:

$$\otimes^k = \left[\underline{a}^k, \overline{a}^k\right]$$

Example: $\otimes \in [2, 4], k = 2, \otimes^2 == [4, 16]$

The presented operations on interval grey numbers are the most commonly used in practical applications. More and more progress is being made in research in this area each year. Currently, attempts are being made to build an algebraic system for grey numbers based on a structure called a grey kernel [5]. This system has been supplemented by a number of systematisation improvements and the introduction of the concept of genereal grey number [6]. Currently, its basic structure is well described and available in the literature [7], pp. 29–43. The grey-kernel-based system, due to the virtues of generality, has great theoretical potential. However, due to practical applications, it is preferable to use classical solutions due to the ease of interpretation of results and intermediate steps of the computational process.

We can interpret grey numbers essentially essentially in two ways. The first is the conceptual approach, i.e. one in which the numbers do not refer to phenomena in the real world. The second approach, on the other hand, is the empirical approach; these numbers refer to some entities existing in empirical reality. Adopting this interpretative distinction, it is reasonable to distinguish two categories of grey numbers: abstract grey numbers and concrete grey numbers [1, 8]. In the case of research and practical applications in the management sciences, there is no doubt that we can only consider concrete grey numbers, as we must have a reference to empirical reality. If, according to the definitional meaning, a grey number in the most general sense is a number from the set of real numbers about which we know only that it is within a certain range, then in the case of grey concrete numbers, the relation linking the number to empirical reality is the distribution of possible values describing the phenomenon in question. This distribution is limited by the lower and upper ranges of the given grey number. On the other hand, the expected value of this distribution will be the whitened value of that number, and the very process of identifying this distribution and determining its expected value will be the process of whitening the grey number. Whitening is fundamental to operations performed on grey numbers and becomes particularly important in the case of sorting and comparison [1]. However, the identification of distributions in the whitening process often poses many difficulties that could undermine the sense of using grey modelling. A solution to this problem is to assume a priori a uniform distribution. The rationale behind such a procedure is that a given grey number can take on any value defined by its range with the same probability. This reflects the realistic assumption that the researcher has no additional knowledge of the object or phenomenon being analysed. He or she is only able to determine the upper and lower limits of a given quantitative characteristic. Furthermore, whether a grey number is discrete or continuous, the expected value is always nothing more than the arithmetic mean. For continuous numbers, it is the arithmetic mean of the upper and lower limits of a given number, while for discrete numbers, it is the arithmetic mean of all values within the range of a given number. This is important insofar as it simplifies analytical operations computationally and interpretatively. However, another more important rationale for adopting a uniform distribution is that such a distribution does not result in a difference at the pragmatic level between the algebraic system of abstract grey numbers and operations on concrete grey numbers. In an ontological sense, of course, these are two worlds: the empirical and the abstract; however, in an applied sense, the numbers are indistinguishable. This indistinguishability means that we can transfer the theoretical achievements associated with the development of grey number algebraic systems to research practice. In other words: this approach combines theory and empiricals.

In the applications of grey numbers in management science research, there are essentially two groups of models. The first of these includes models that we can call hybrid models based on grey numbers. On the second hand, we can include models in which grey numbers are used to transform evaluations expressed on linguistic scales into scales of a quantitative nature.

The main idea behind the group of hybrid models based on grey numbers is the integration of grey numbers with known analytical models. Here, it is important to signal that hybrid models represent a broader group of methods that can use other GST methods in addition to grey numbers. This will be discussed more extensively in the following discussion in Sect. 4.5. A common feature of hybrid models based on grey numbers is the replacement of operations on precisely defined real numbers by grey algebraic operations. This need arises from the high complexity of the phenomena under study in management systems, where the determination of exact and precise values of variables in the quantification process raises many methodological, cost, and organisational difficulties. Examples of well-known models in which grey numbers have been successfully applied include: classical decision-making models [9–12], models based on game theory [13], models based on neural networks, models based on rough set theory [14] or models based on fuzzy logic [15–19]. The range of applications of these models follows the range of applications of the original models, which were subject to grey modification. The only extension is that resulting from the grey representation of the data in terms of grey numbers. Here, it is also worth signaling an important methodological point regarding the integration of the grey approach with other methodological solutions. In this respect, the imperative should be the principle that methodological integration should not be attempted when we deliberately and artificially need to informationally weaken the data so that grey numbers can be used. Furthermore, it is highly questionable to integrate classical statistical methods with modelling using grey numbers. Statistical models model precise data, and in the end the results should also be precise. This is not possible when using grey numbers. The uncertainty of grey numbers is limited by the lower and upper bounds of the number. Therefore, in many cases in statistical models where a specific conclusive value is needed, its derivation in the whitening process may be arbitrary and introduce additional ambiguity in the interpretation of the results. An example is the verification of statistical hypotheses. The use of grey numbers means that the result of the test statistic calculation will also be a grey number. Comparing then such a result with the critical value may not give a clear decision whether to accept or reject the hypothesis in question. Even using a procedure to whittle down the final result, another problem will arise: How to determine the power of such a test? Examples of this type with regard to statistical methods can be multiplied, the underlying reason being the inability to obtain precise results from imprecise data. This consideration should also be taken to a large extent with other methods where grey numbers are used, but in the case of statistical approaches, the use of grey numbers implies problems at a fundamental interpretative level. In other cases, where the data collected at the input are imprecise and therefore the obtaining of imprecise final and intermediate results in the calculations is inherent in the analytical process itself, grey numbers are then a convenient way of representing a certain type of uncertainty and do not interfere in any way with the interpretation, since from the very beginning of the analysis the researcher is aware of the methodological limitations that he or she can minimise by triangulation, resorting to qualitative methods or expert knowledge.

The essence of the second group of models that use grey numbers in management science research is the quantification of linguistic features by assigning them a quantity feature expressed in terms of grey numbers. From an application point of view, this process means that the scope of application of grey systems theory can be analogous to fuzzy logic. An important question arises here: when to choose grey modelling and when to choose fuzzy logic? We should choose grey modelling when there is no knowledge of the membership function, or the form of such a function is difficult to determine, and standard triangular or trapezoidal functions are arbitrary and difficult to justify in the context of the problem at hand. Otherwise, it is far better to adopt a fuzzy approach to modelling the problem.

The transformation of linguistic features into a set of grey numbers, despite its importance, has not received an in-depth theoretical analysis in the literature. This can be done with the help of the kvalitological notion of feature and feature state and functional relations on sets.

Let us therefore assume that we have any linguistic feature L for which a set of its states has been identified and formulated $S(L)$ in a given natural language. Moreover, let us assume that on the set of $S(L)$ a valuing relation has been introduced R, which transforms the set into an ascendingly ordered set (3.1):

$$\{S(L), R\} = \{l_1, \ldots, l_n\} \tag{2.1}$$

Let us also assume that we have a given set consisting of interval grey numbers $\otimes S$ and assume that this set is also ascendingly ordered, which can be written as follows (3.2):

$$\{\otimes S, \leq\} = \{\otimes_1, \ldots \otimes_k\} \tag{2.2}$$

In order to put this set in order $\otimes S$ it is necessary to perform a grey number comparison operation. This problem is not trivial in grey systems theory and has received various in-depth theoretical treatments of the issue [1, 8, 20], [21–23]. However, considering the pragmatic criterion, it is recommended that the process be the most intuitive and computationally simplest. Hence, assuming that we are dealing with concrete grey numbers with a uniform distribution, it is easy to determine the expected value, which is the arithmetic mean of the upper and lower limits of a given grey number. The expected value from a uniform distribution for a given grey number is often referred to in the literature as the kernel of grey number [5, 6]. It makes it possible to easily compare and sort grey numbers despite possible caveats due to current theoretical advances in grey number algebraic systems.

In the process of transforming the states of linguistic features into grey numbers, the foundation of this process is to use a pattern that will explicitly define the rules for assigning the linguistic states of a given feature the corresponding grey number. Such a pattern can be written in functional form, and we can call it a transformation function. Therefore, let us assume that the function F is given by formula (2.3):

$$F : \{S(L), R\} \to \{\otimes S, \leq\} \tag{2.3}$$

The function F will be a transformation function if it satisfies the following conditions:

- The function must be a bijection mapping the set $\{S(L), R\}$ into the set $\{\otimes S, \leq\}$
- for each $l_i, l_j \in \{S(L), R\} j \geq i$ and $F(l_i) = \otimes_s$ $F(l_j) = \otimes_m$ the following relation holds: $\otimes_m \geq \otimes_s$

Intuitively, the conditions shown can be interpreted as follows: For the states of a given linguistic feature that have been ordered in ascending order using some kind of value relation, grey numbers are assigned. Since the transformation function is a bijection, each element from the set of states of the linguistic feature is prescribed exactly one and only one grey number. The assumption of bijection also implies the equality of the sets on which the transformation function is defined, which in effect gives us an exhaustive and unambiguous transformation pattern. In other words, on the basis of the relations between grey numbers, the ordering between the states of the linguistic feature under analysis can be unambiguously reconstructed.

In practical applications, an additional set of the following conditions is introduced:

- for any given element $\otimes_i \in \left[\overline{a_i}, \underline{a_i}\right]$ from the set $\{\otimes S, \leq\} = \{\otimes_1, \ldots \otimes_k\}$ the relation $\overline{a_i} \geq 0$, $\underline{a_i} \geq 0$
- for any given pair $\otimes_s \in [\underline{a_s}, \overline{a_s}]$ $\otimes_m \in [\underline{a_m}, \overline{a_m}]$. , derived from the set $\{\otimes S, \leq\} = \{\otimes_1, \ldots \otimes_k\}$ the following relation holds $\overline{a_s} - \underline{a_s} = \overline{a_m} - \underline{a_m}$
- for any given pair $\otimes_s \in [\underline{a_s}, \overline{a_s}]$ $\otimes_m \in [\underline{a_m}, \overline{a_m}]$ such that $m > s$ the relation $\underline{a_m} - \overline{a_s} = 0$

These intuitive assumptions express the idea that the linguistictates of the features will be mapped into grey numbers in such a way that these numbers exhaustively and uniformly cover some kind of numerical continuum. This continuum is, therefore, the basis and range from which the grey numbers will be taken for transformation.

To better illustrate this point, let us assume that we have a given linguistic feature, which we can synthetically refer to as a 'value judgement.' This feature has the following states:

$$\{S(L), R\} = \{very\ bad, bad, average, good, very\ good\}$$

Let us also assume that the continuum on which the individual states will be mapped into a set of grey numbers has this form:

$$\{\otimes S, \leq\} = \{[0,0;0,2],[0,2;0,4],[0,4;0,6],[0,6;0,8],[0,8;1,0]\}$$

With these two sets, a function can be defined $F : \{S(L), R\} \to \{\otimes S, \leq\}$. The function F in tabular form is shown in Table 2.1.

The function shown in this table satisfies additional conditions related to the exhaustive coverage of the continuum from 0 to 1. Furthermore, each element of the $F(l_i)$ is such that it is non-empty and inseparable from another. It is also worth noting that the verbal formula of the feature 'value judgement' itself is universal in nature

Table 2.1 Tabular representation of the transformation function

Status of the linguistic feature (l_i)	Function value $F(l_i)$
very bad	[0, 0; 0, 2]
bad	[0, 2; 0, 4]
average	[0, 4; 0, 6]
good	[0, 6; 0, 8]
very good	[0, 8; 1, 0]

and can have a wide range, i.e. it can be attributed to a large number of items. Its use in this sense, therefore, has a high degree of universality. The transformative function F on this attribute can also be referred to as a scale or pattern of evaluation. Of course, the general form of the transformation function also offers the possibility of generating an issue-specific pattern, taking into account the uniqueness of the nature of the analysed object. Then, such a pattern will have a limited scope of application; however, it may be more precise in rendering the specific elements of the evaluation that the researcher cares about.

An interesting issue related to the generation of patterns or scales is the problem of appropriately identifying the states of a trait. Logically we can treat a verbal evaluation formula as a name. Such a procedure causes the problem of identifying states of a given linguistic feature to be treated as a problem of logical classification of a given name. As a result of such a classification, we should obtain an exhaustive and closed division of the scope of a given name into subsets that are nonempty and disjoint. Another problem that needs to be signalled is that, despite the identification of a set of states of a given characteristic with logical rigour, when using a rating pattern or scale, users interpret the given verbal formulas differently at the semantic level. Some verbal formulas for users may be fuzzy. For example, it can be difficult in some cases to grasp the difference between very good and good or between bad and very bad. How can this therefore be modelled using the function F? The answer to the question posed in this way is related to negating the separability of the grey numbers forming the set of $\{\otimes S, \leq\}$ and by abandoning the assumption that all ranges of these numbers are equal to each other. This approach creates a common area for the integration of grey and fuzzy modelling.

In summary, the basic direction of modelling problems using grey numbers in the context of management science is related to extending the capabilities of existing methodological and analytical procedures to include the issue of uncertainty associated with quantitative proxies. Additionally, grey numbers can be very useful in constructing scales and evaluation patterns. Due to the flexibility of algebraic operations on them, results from such scales can be easily interpreted and analysed.

2.2 Grey Incidence Analysis in Management Research

Models that examine the relationships between variables are collectively called grey incidence analysis (GIA) in grey systems theory. These models have a similar scope of application to regression analysis or the study of correlations in the statistical approach. However, the difference between grey and statistical approaches is that GIA models do not require assumptions about the size of the data set held and do not require assumptions about knowledge of the distribution of the characteristics under study in the general population. Often, therefore, statistical conclusions due to the restrictive nature of the assumptions can be unreliable and contradictory to a qualitative analysis. In GIA models, the small empirical base and the lack of knowledge of distributions are not a hindrance to research, as the correct application of these models requires the use of qualitative analysis and a multidimensional, not just quantitative, understanding of the phenomenon under study at the initial stage of research. This approach is a result of the fact that GIA models are usually used to analyse complex systems such as economic or management systems. Therefore, the methodology of their use must take into account the social science paradigm. Relating this methodology to the paradigms and research strategies previously discussed in the management sciences, we can conclude that the GIA approach is consistent with them, especially in the context of complementing quantitative research with qualitative research, thus making good on the demands of methodological triangulation.

We can essentially reduce the research process using GIA methods to five stages, which are:

- Systemic conceptualisation of the study, the essence of which is to define the objectives of the study and the scope of the study. In addition, it is fundamental at this stage to define the subject of the study in systemic terms, i.e. the given problem should be defined in such a way that it is possible to determine unambiguously which aspects of the problem are taken into account in the study and which are deliberately omitted and reduced.
- Qualitative modelling of the system under study, the main objective of which is to identify the relevant features of this system from the point of view of the given study and the relationships that take place in this system. The result of this stage is a qualitative and structured model of the given problem described linguistically.
- Quantification of the system under study, which aims to transform a qualitative model into a quantitative model so that empirical quantitative data can be collected.
- Selection of an appropriate analytical model and analysis of the data using formal procedures specific to the GIA model.
- Systematic validation of the study, where the aim of this validation is to continuously adapt the research process to the changing structure of the problem being analysed and its context, as well as the structure and conditions of the research itself.

These steps are necessary from the point of view of the research methodology for GIA models to be successfully applied in management science research. However, a common methodological mistake is to focus in modelling with GIA on issues related to the mathematical formalism, thus omitting many important elements of the research procedure. An omitted or superficial approach to qualitative analysis in GIA can result in a negative assessment of the methodological soundness of the research. This problem can be seen when the researcher claims that it is possible to draw general conclusions from the research through formal mathematical procedures. Once again, it should be strongly emphasised that it is the empirical base that determines the level of generalisability of the results, not the properties of the analytical method. With a small empirical base in GIA models, it is possible to capture the relationships that occur, but their generalisation requires plausibility according to the assumptions of methodological triangulation.

Because GIA models use white number data sequences, we can classify them as models based on a distributive understanding of grey. Therefore, the analysis of the data in these models requires preprocessing of the data using special operators that transform the raw data. As a rule, five standard operators are used in classical GIA models. Their set can be written as follows:

$$D = \{D_i | i = 1, 2, 3, 4, 5\}$$

We call this set the set of grey incidence operators. In order to formally describe the operation of the individual operators, let us assume that we have the original data sequence:

$$X_i = (x_i(1), x_i(2) \ldots x_i(n))$$

The operator D_1 is called the inintialing operator and transforms the original data sequence as follows:

$$X_i D_1 = (x_i(1)d_1, x_i(2)d_1 \ldots x_i(n)d_1) \text{ Where : } x_i(k)d_1 = \frac{x_i(k)}{x_i(1)}$$

The operator D_2 is called the averaging operator and transforms the original data sequence as follows:

$$X_i D_2 = (x_i(1)d_2, x_i(2)d_2 \ldots x_i(n)d_2) \text{ Where : } x_i(k)d_2 = \frac{x_i(k)}{\frac{1}{n}\sum_i^n x_i(k)}$$

The operator D_3 is called the interval operator and transforms the original data sequence as follows:

$$X_i D_3 = (x_i(1)d_3, x_i(2)d_3 \ldots x_i(n)d_3) \text{ Where : } x_i(k)d_3 = \frac{x_i(k) - \min\{x_i(k)\}}{\max\{x_i(k)\} - \min\{x_i(k)\}}$$

The operator D_4 can only be shuffled in a data sequence for which the following assumption is maintained: $x_i(k) = [0, 1]$. This operator is called the reversing operator (reversing operator) and transforms the original data sequence as follows:

$$X_i D_4 = (x_i(1)d_4, x_i(2)d_4 \ldots x_i(n)d_4) \text{Where : } x_i(k)d_4 = 1 - x_i(k)$$

The operator D_5 is called the reciprocating operator and transforms the original data sequence as follows:

$$X_i D_5 = (x_i(1)d_5, x_i(2)d_5 \ldots x_i(n)d_5) \text{ Where : } x_i(k)d_5 = \frac{1}{x_i(k)}$$

Operators D_1, D_2, D_3 are intended to transform the original data sequences into sequences of titer-free data. As a rule, they should be combined with great care in practical applications. The choice of operator is of great importance for the results obtained. Hence, its selection should be preceded by a thorough analysis by the researcher. For example, the use of the operator D_1 may make sense in the case of a time sequence, where the first element of the sequence is the output value of some index to which subsequent data in the sequence relate. The operator D_2 on the other hand, bases its transformation on the arithmetic mean of the data values in the sequence. This operator can be applied to sequences of data characterising some phenomenon or objects against a given set of criteria, where GIA is used in evaluation or decision-making processes. The operator D_3 in turn normalises the values of the original sequence to a set between 0 and 1. This operator, like the operator D_2 is indicated in applications for decision-making or evaluation processes. However, it should be emphasised that the operators D_2 and D_3 in addition to their specific applications, can also be used for temporal sequences when there is no substantive indication of any preference for the first item in the data sequence. The operators D_4 i D_5 Operators allow a given data sequence to be modelled when the feature being analysed is a minimant, i.e. the lower the value, the better from the point of view of some valuing criterion. In the case of a minmanta, a transformation is often needed to change the direction of the valuation of a given feature. In other words, when we have a given primary sequence X_i and it is negatively correlated withX_j, then after transforming X_j using the operator D_4 or D_5 sequence $X_j D_4$ or $X_j D_5$ will already be positively correlated withX_j. The set of operators presented earlier D is the canonical set and traditionally the one most commonly used in GIA models. It should be noted, however, that there is nothing to prevent one from reaching for other data transformations developed from grey systems theory and data mining and statistics.

There are a number of models categorised as GIAs. There has been intensive theoretical and application development in this field for many years. A detailed overview, classifications, and evaluation of the effectiveness of different approaches in this field can be found in the literature [7], pp. 21–23; [24, 25]. In addition, there are emerging studies focussing on the weaknesses of the grey relational approach, especially in evaluative and decision-making contexts [2]. These are important insofar as they not only draw attention to the mathematical aspects of GIA, but also raise important methodological issues. As a rule, however, the most dominant model in applications is the classical model developed by Deng [26] based on point distance and a group of surface models [27].

The starting point in the classical GIA model is the identification of data sequences X_0 reflecting the characteristics of a given system and a sequence of data X_i describing the factors influencing these characteristics. Formally, these data sequences can be written as follows.

$$X_0 = (x_0(1), x_0(2) \ldots x_0(n))$$
$$X_i = (x_i(1), x_i(2) \ldots x_i(n))i = 1, 2 \ldots .m$$

In the first step of determining the relationship index between X_0 a X_i an appropriate operator should be applied D, taking into account the specifics of the analysis to be carried out. This will result in the following new data sequences:

$$X_0' = (x_0'(1), x_0'(2) \ldots x_0'(n)) \text{ where } X_0' = X_0 D;\ x_0'(k) = x_0(k)d$$
$$X_i' = (x_i'(1), x_i'(2) \ldots x_i'(n)) \text{ where } X_i' = X_i D;\ x_i'(k) = x_i(k)d$$

The sequences of differential data should then be determined $\Delta_i = (\Delta_i(1), \Delta_i(2) \ldots . \Delta_i(n))$:

$$\Delta_i(k) = \left|x_0'(k) - x_i'(k)\right|$$

With the sequence Δ_i, in the next step it is possible to determine the coefficient of relationship coefficient between X_0 a X_i. Denoting this coefficient γ_{0i}, we calculate it in such a way that we first determine its values at the individual points k:

$$\gamma_{0i}(k) = \frac{m + \rho M}{\Delta_i(k) + \rho M}$$

where:
$M = \max \Delta_i(k)$
$m = \min \Delta_i(k)$
$\rho \in (0, 1)$ - an arbitrarily and arbitrarily chosen value, usually assumed to be 0.5 when there is no additional indication or information.

Then, having the values $\gamma_{0i}(k)$, we calculate the arithmetic mean from them. We then obtain the final result, which we write down formally as follows.

$$\gamma_{0i} = \sum_{k=1}^{n} \gamma_{0i}(k)\, i = 1, 2 \ldots m$$

This indicator is called the degree of incidence. It has the following important properties:

- It is standardised, i.e.: $0 < \gamma_{0i} \leq 1$ i.e.: the closer the value γ_{0i} is closer to 1, the higher the level of relationship between the data sequences, with the indicator never reaching 0, which can be interpreted to mean that each data sequence is always at least minimally correlated.
- It is not globally symmetric, i.e. for any $X_i, X_j \in X$ where: $X = \{X_1, X_2 \ldots X_m\}$ and $m > 2$ the following relation holds $\gamma_{ij} \neq \gamma_{ji}$ $(i \neq j)$.
- It is symmetrical only in pairs, i.e. $\gamma_{ij} = \gamma_{ji} \iff X_i, X_j \in X$ and $X = \{X_i, X_j\}$.
- It is an indicator based on the proximity of data at particular points k in such a way that the smaller the values $\Delta_i(k)$ values, the higher the value of this indicator.

In mathematical terms, the degree of incidence can be seen as a way of examining the relationship between the observation vectors of some complex system. The study of this relationship consists in determining the similarity of the geometric shape of the vectors. However, this indicator does not take into account the position of the vectors in space.

Within the group of surface GIA models, one of the most popular models is undoubtedly the absolute degree of grey incidence model. It examines in an isolated manner always two sequences of data depicting the behaviour of the system. For the purposes of further consideration, let us assume that these are X_i and X_j :

$$X_i = (x_i(1), x_i(2) \dots x_i(n))$$
$$X_j = \left(x_j(1), x_j(2) \dots x_j(n)\right)$$

Data sequences X_i and X_j illustrate the behaviour of the system at particular moments of observation $k = 1, 2 \dots .n$. In the first step of determining the absolute degree of grey incidence, the original data sequence must be transformed using a special zero starting point operator. It transforms the data in such a way that it subtracts the value of the starting position from each data in the sequence. We then obtain new data sequences X_i^0 and X_j^0. Formally, the operation of this operator can be written as follows:

$$X_i^0 = (x_i(1) - x_i(1), x_i(2) - x_i(1) \dots x_i(n) - x_i(n))$$
$$X_j^0 = \left(x_j(1) - x_j(1), x_j(2) - x_j(2) \dots x_j(n) - x_j(1)\right)$$

Intepretting this transformation geometrically, it is possible to imagine a set of broken lines whose origin is at point 0. Using sequences of X_i^0 and X_j^0, we determine the following intermediate indices:

$$|s_i| = \left|\sum_{k=2}^{n-1} x_i^0(k) + \frac{1}{2}x_i^0(n)\right|$$

$$\left|s_j\right| = \left|\sum_{k=2}^{n-1} x_j^0(k) + \frac{1}{2}x_j^0(n)\right|$$

$$\left|s_i - s_j\right| = \left|\sum_{k=2}^{n-1}[x_i^0(k) - x_j^0(k)] + \frac{1}{2}[x_i^0(n) - x_j^0(n)]\right|$$

With the intermediate indicators determined, it is possible to determine the absolute degree of grey incidence ε_{ij} according to the formula:

$$\varepsilon_{ij} = \frac{1 + |s_i| + \left|s_j\right|}{1 + |s_i| + \left|s_j\right| - \left|s_i - s_j\right|}$$

A detailed discussion of the mathematical properties of the indicator ε_{ij} and the presentation of formal proofs are shown in the literature [3], pp. 101–112, [4], pp. 76–81. From the point of view of the analysis of complex systems such as management systems, much more important than formal and mathematical considerations and properties are the following conclusions about the interpretation of the indicator ε_{ij} [28], pp. 14–15):

- The indicator is normalised, i.e.$0 < \varepsilon_{ij} \leq 1$
- The higher the value of the indicator, the higher the degree of association between the sequences of data analysed.
- Any two vectors are always at least minimally related, as the index never takes the value 0.
- If the data sequences are parallel or fluctuate around each other, the $\varepsilon_{ij} = 1$
- There is an identity relation such that: $\varepsilon_{ii} = \varepsilon_{jj} = 1$ and a symmetry relation such that: $\varepsilon_{ij} = \varepsilon_{ji}$,

The properties of an indicator $\varepsilon_{ij.}$ and especially its symmetry, can be used to classify and group objects or variables. A model using this property in this way is called grey clusters of grey incidences [3], pp. 140–144. This indicator can also be used to analyse preferences and determine the order of importance of factors in a complex system in relation to the identified characteristics of that system [3], pp. 120–132.

As indicated earlier, the absolute degree of grey incidence index is one of many surface models. It is popular in practical and scientific applications. However, it should be noted for the sake of argument that a very similar indicator is the relative degree of grey incidence. The mechanism for its determination is very similar to ε_{ij}, with the difference being in the way the data are preprocessed, involving the use of a different grey operator. Another interesting surface indicator worth mentioning is the synthetic indicator, which is a combination of an absolute indicator and a relative indicator. A detailed discussion of the formal construction of these indicators and their properties is available in the basic monographs on grey systems [3].

Grey modelling by means of GIA in the context of management science should not be regarded as an alternative to correlational statistical methods. This becomes particularly relevant in the case of sample surveys. The large amount of data and the high quality of the data required in these surveys should incline towards statistical methods.

The GIA approach is based on the paradigm of systems analysis, an inherent feature of which is the combination of multiple research perspectives, particularly qualitative and quantitative analysis. In research strategies in which the criterion of the reality of the context in which the object or phenomenon under study operates is important and a nonrigorous and systemic approach to the set of variables under study is assumed, GIA models can be successfully applied. The set of problems that can be clarified thanks to them can be reduced to the following questions.

- Which factors are most important for a given complex system? This is a question of ranking a set of factors in terms of their importance from a cognitive and causal point of view in management processes.
- What factors have a decisive influence on the development of a problem, process, or complex system? This is a question about developmental trends in organisations and management systems.

- What factors in the current state of a given system and its context influence the desired and negative direction of a given system? In other words, it is a question of how to direct management signals in order to reinforce pro-development factors and control factors that may pose risks to the organisation.

The catalogue of possible research problems indicated is open. However, it is important to note that in the case of socio-technical systems, they are difficult to structure and quantify, and therefore a purely quantitative analysis without taking into account the heuristic, qualitative, and systemic aspects may oversimplify the reality under study or only be possible in the analysis of trivial issues, which from a scientific and practical point of view is of little use.

2.3 Grey Forecasting Models in Management Research

Grey predictive models are one of the most important issues being developed within GST. They allow us to map the dynamics of the behaviour of the system under study on the basis of a very sparse time series. The simplest grey predictive model is one in which we can observe the behaviour of a given system only by observing its one output. The construction of a predictive model in such a case can be reduced to the following few steps [3], pp. 197–217, [28], pp. 12–14:

Step 1 In this step, a vector of observations is acquired for the analysed output in the system. In this model, it is important that the observation values are not negative and the minimum length of the vector should be at least four elements. We can formally write this vector as follows:

$$x^{(0)} = (x^{(0)}(1), x^{(0)}(2), \ldots x^{(0)}(n))$$

Step 2 In this step, the observation vector will be transformed using the AGO (accumulating generation operators). This smooths out the information noise in the model resulting from the randomness of the data. The operation of the AGO operator can be formally written as follows:

$$x^{(1)} = AGO\big((x^{(0)}(1), x^{(0)}(2), \ldots x^{(0)}(n))\big)$$

$$x^{(1)} = (x^{(1)}(1), x^{(2)}(2), \ldots x^{(2)}(n)),\ \text{where}: \ x^{(1)}(k) = \sum_{i=1}^{k} x^{(0)}(i)\ k = 1, 2 \ldots n$$

Step 3 In this step, we formulate the form of the predictive model. Given that the observation vector and the vector smoothed by the AGO operator are a representation of the system behaviour as a function of time, we can formulate the following differential equation:

$$\frac{dx^{(1)}}{dt} = ax^{(1)}(t) = u$$

Step 4 In this step, the form of the solution of the differential equation is determined. This solution has the following form:

$$\hat{x}^{(1)}(k+1) = \left[x^{(0)}(1) - \frac{u}{a}\right]e^{-ak} + \frac{u}{a}$$

Step 5 In this step, the parameters are determined a and u. This can be done by replacing the differential equation with a system of differential equations and reducing it to matrix form.

$$[a, u] = (B^T B)^{-1} B^T Y$$

where:

$$Y = [(x^{(0)}(2), x^{(0)}(3), \ldots x^{(0)}(n))]^T$$

$$B = \begin{bmatrix} -0,5[x^{(1)}(1) + x^{(1)}(2)] & 1 \\ -0,5[x^{(1)}(2) + x^{(1)}(3)] & 1 \\ \ldots & \ldots \\ -0,5[x^{(1)}(n-1) + x^{(1)}(n)] & 1 \end{bmatrix}$$

Step 5 In this step, we determine the value of the forecast by an inverse operation to the AGO operator, i.e., by subtracting successive forecasts of smoothed vectors, doing so as follows:

$$\hat{x}^{(0)}(k+1) = \hat{x}^{(0)}(k+1) - \hat{x}^{(0)}(k)$$
$$\hat{x}^{(0)}(k+1) = \left[x^{(0)}(1) - \tfrac{u}{a}\right](e^{-ak} - e^{-(k-1)})$$

Furthermore, in this step, the forecast error for the model can also be determined ε as follows:

$$\varepsilon = \hat{x}^{(0)}(k) - x^{(0)}(k)$$

The model shown is called GM(1,1). The first number in the notation suggests that it is a first-order differential model, and the second number informs us that the model has one output variable. In other words, the notation indicates that from a mathematical point of view, the predictive model takes the form of a first-order differential equation with one variable. This model, proposed by [29], is a basic model and one of the most widely used in grey forecasting. Of course, the theoretical progress related to the development of higher-order models, the way data are collected and processed, and with more variables is enormous, and its historical complexity, especially in the application aspect, is multidisciplinary in nature [30]. When analysing grey predictive models, it is important to note that, as a rule, the data needed for the model are sequences of white numbers. There are, of course, attempts to develop predictive models for grey number sequences [31, 32]. However, they do not represent a major direction in the research agenda for predictive methods in grey systems theory. This state of affairs entitles us to classify predictive methods into a group of issues in grey systems theory related to the distributive distribution of grey. Hence, in the first step in the construction of grey forecasting models, the issue of appropriate smoothing of data with the help of grey operators comes to the fore.

Grey predictive models have found several applications in management science research [33–36]. Of course, in the literature, one can find the use of the word management in many grey forecasting articles, e.g. electricity market or demand. However, this can hardly be regarded as problems typical of contemporary considerations in this field of knowledge. Rather, it has the character of a certain fashion and stylistic and linguistic convention, rather than a conscious reference to the scope of research problems of organisation and management theory. The low popularity of grey forecasting models in managerial applications is due to the dynamic and complex nature of management problems. Attempting to forecast variables in such phenomena in coordinate time, based on historical data, is methodologically questionable. The question then arises: What methodological assumptions should be made to make grey forecasting models useful in management science? The answer can be reduced to the following statements:

- Grey predictive models are embedded in a systems approach, so any problem or phenomenon analysed should be formulated using the conceptual apparatus of systems analysis. This aspect should generally be an integrative imperative of grey systems theory and management science in terms of the neo-positivist functional-systems paradigm.
- Grey forecasting models, in order to be useful, must be constantly validated against new incoming information on the functioning of the system under analysis; this validation, in addition to the influx of new data into the time series, should also take into account qualitative data on the structure of the system, the context in which it functions, and the energy, material, and information inputs and outputs of the system.
- Grey forecasting models can be very useful when there are data gaps in a given time series; then they can be reasonably supplemented by a model based on the available empirical base.
- Grey forecasting models can describe patterns and trends in the system under analysis, but should never be taken as an accurate forecast of the future; these models should be interpreted qualitatively, as a potential direction of development of some system.
- Grey forecasting models are built on the basis of mechanisms and relationships that have been operated in the past, which does not imply that these relationships will be repeated in the future.

In summary, forecasting detailed values of variables in any management system has many epistemological limitations. However, forecasting methods should not be completely dismissed in management applications, as they can provide useful knowledge about current and past organisational trends and existing directions of change in the environment. Such research is usually carried out in a comprehensive manner in forward-looking analyses based on the assumptions of foresight methodologies [37–39]. These studies can be very useful for rational decision-making and can be a means of minimising uncertainty in managerial activities. Grey forecasting models, despite their mathematical and quantitative sophistication, should therefore be more of an inspiration for in-depth qualitative studies on the future than an attempt to determine it objectively and precisely.

2.4 Grey Decision Making Models in Support of Management Processes

In the most general sense, we can treat management as a complex information and decision-making process realised in sociotechnical systems. In this sense, the essence of managers' work is to make accurate decisions with regard to the resources subordinate to them in the context of all management functions. Decisions may therefore concern: planning issues, the selection and organisation of resources in relation to set goals, motivation issues, or issues related to managerial control issues. Thus, it can be hypothesised that decision-making is a metafunction of management, as it is always manifested in the other functions of management, i.e. planning, organising, motivating, and controlling [40], pp. 110–117, [41]. Decision-making processes are therefore of fundamental importance in management science. As such, they are the subject of advanced interdisciplinary research at the interface of psychology, cognitive science, mathematics, economics, or operations research [42], pp. 51–52.

The starting point in the decision-making process is the identification of a decision problem, i.e. a situation in which an acting entity (the decision-maker) becomes aware and then structures a situation in which it has to make a choice. On the other hand, by decision itself, we can understand the act of choosing before the decision maker between at least two different acceptable options on the basis of the decision criteria adopted. The purpose of decision making is to select the optimal option in a given decision-making situation. Adopting the distinction, known from analytical philosophy, between actions and the results of these actions [43, 44], we can say that a decision is the result of a decision-making process [42], p. 51.

The concepts of choice and decision need to be clarified. Choice is a broader concept than decision. It does not have to be justified or rationalised by any criterion. It can be made entirely arbitrarily [45], pp. 37–41. Such choices usually concern problems related to a value system, a system of needs, or aesthetic issues. Of course, such a choice is a completely free internal act of the subject, but the consequences of the choice are already subject to the rules of the external world. Decision-making, on the other hand, must always be rationalised. The rationale for this rationalisation can be the decision criteria, on the one hand, and the environment in which the decision is made, on the other. The choice of criteria is usually influenced by the decision maker, while the elements of the environment have little or no influence. Therefore, they are treated as boundary conditions in the decision-making process. A special case of decisions is intuitive decisions made and rationalised by the intuition of the decision-maker. This criterion is eminently subjective; however, in practical activities, it often plays a fundamental role in decision-making processes [46–50]. Intuitive decision making based on tacit and unconscious knowledge is a psychological problem, while decision making based on clear rationales linked logically to the goal and boundary conditions of the decision is a praxeological issue. Undoubtedly, decision support methods in GST refer to a praxeological view of the issue. They are not intuitive methods or refer to complex defendant heuristics.

Grey decision methods are the most diverse group of methods in GST. One can find methods referring to various forms of grey information expression from grey numbers to the whitening function, to the distributive understanding of grey. Furthermore, there is a great deal of methodological eclecticism in the field of grey decision-making methods, which makes it difficult to resolve what can be considered a grey systems method and what is only loosely related to the grey approach. In principle, however, the division of decision-making methods in GST can be made into the following three groups [3], p. 358:

- Methods designed for the mass decision-maker, where we have a large group of decision-makers with a low level of responsibility for decisions and diffuse or incomplete knowledge of the decision problem.
- Methods designed for the expert decision-maker, where we have a medium-sized group of decision-makers, with a high level of responsibility for detailed and operational issues and a relatively high level of knowledge on the decision problem team.
- Methods designed for the administrative decision-maker, where we have a small group of decision-makers, with a high level of organisational power and a high level of knowledge about the decision-making process, with a particular focus on opportunities, risks, and the potential to implement the decision taken.

Methods designed for the mass decision-maker can be used in modelling management decision-making situations when it is a matter of taking into account the opinions and experiences of lower hierarchical operational staff in decision-making. This aspect is extremely important in a participative model of organisational management and in building appropriate relationships with internal stakeholders in the organisation. Methods intended for the expert decision-maker, on the other hand, can be used in modelling decision-making situations, where it is important to identify existing development trends and technological or organisational changes. Methods intended for the administrative decision-maker are those where a balance is needed between the current state in the organisation and future trends, while taking into account legal, economic, ethical or environmental restrictions and obligations.

The presented division of decision-making methods in GST integrates well with the division of management in an organisation into operational, tactical, and strategic levels. It is clearly more transparent in the context of management science than the approach based on the criterion of the form of expression of grey information [42, 51] or the traditional division resulting from the mathematical structure of the decision model [3]. Due to the extremely large scope of decision-making issues in GST, as well as the great variety of methods and the systematic activity of researchers in this field, the methods representative of the group of methods in the adopted and discussed classification will be presented in more detail in the following discussion.

In the group of methods designed for the mass decision maker, the representative method is the grey statistical decision method [3], pp. 341–347, [52, 53]. In it, data are derived from a large group of decision makers and then synthesised to agree on the classification of options into specific decision groups. This method uses a whitening function to model the preferences of decision makers. The model can be reduced to the following steps:

Step 1 Organisation of the decision-making group of decision-makers $A = \{a_1, a_2, \ldots a_n\}$ and identification of a set of decision-making options $B = \{b_1, b_2, \ldots, b_m\}$

Step 2 Determine the importance of individual decision makers η_i, where $\sum_{i=1}^{n} \eta_i = 1$. Determining validity can be an optional step and omitted if there are a large number of decision-makers, as then there is a blurring of validity.

Step 3 Determination of the whitening function $f^k(x_{ij})$, where: $k = 1, 2, \ldots, s$ denotes the whitening function for the decision class. The number of classes can be freely chosen depending on the specific decision situation.

Step 4 In this step, each decision-maker a_i assesses each option b_j. This assessment can be written as x_{ij}, where: $i = 1, 2, \ldots n$; $j = 1, 2, \ldots, m$.

Step 5 Determine the decision factor as follows:

$$\sigma_j^k = \frac{\sum_{i=1}^{n} f^k(x_{ij}) \cdot \eta_i}{\sum_{k=1}^{s} \sum_{i=1}^{n} f^k(x_{ij}) \cdot \eta_i}$$

Step 6 Determine the decision vector for each decision option as follows:

$$\sigma_j = \left(\sigma_j^1, \sigma_j^2, \ldots \sigma_j^s\right)$$

Step 7 Classify the individual decision options into the defined decision classes as follows:

$$\max\{\sigma_j^k\} = \sigma_j^{k^*}$$

Classification of individual variants is done by means of a superscript k^* in such a way that it indicates that the variant a_j has been classified into a decision class k^*.

The model presented does not select a single best-decision option, but classifies all identified options into groups. The decision groups should be defined to reflect the order on the basis of some value criterion such as the cost of implementing the option, the difficulty of implementing the option, or the time needed for implementation. How groups are ordered depends on the specific decision-making process. However, given the general methodological aspects of GST, it is a reasonable recommendation to validate the model with qualitative methods.

In the group of methods designed for the expert decision maker, a representative model is the Grey Development Decisions model [3, 54, 55]. It uses the classical predictive model of GM (1,1) on the one hand, but advanced expert knowledge is needed to benefit from its application. The model first requires an analytical definition of the decision-making situation in the event-measures context. The set of events belongs to elements that are independent of the decision maker, while the measures are significantly influenced by the decision maker. Formally, the set of decision-making situations S can be expressed as follows [3], pp. 316–318:

$$S = \left\{s_{ij} = \left(a_i, b_j\right)\right\} a_i \in A, b_i \in B$$

where:

$A = \{a_1, a_2, \ldots, a_n\}$- we call the set of events
$B = \{b_1, b_2, \ldots, b_m\}$- we call the set of remedies.

With an analytically defined set of events, the Grey Development Decisions model can be reduced to a sequence of the following steps [3], pp. 336–341):

Step 1 Identify the time sequence of states of each decision situation s_{ij} with respect to the adopted *decision* criterion k, which can be formally written as follows:

$$u_{ij}^{(k)} = \left(u_{ij}^{(k)}(1), u_{ij}^{(k)}(2), \ldots, u_{ij}^{(k)}(h)\right)$$

Step 2 For the specified time sequence in this step, the model will be built $GM(1, 1)$. Its parameters will be as follows:

$$\hat{a}_{ij}^{(k)} = \left[a_{ij}^{(k)}, b_{ij}^{(k)}\right]^T$$

With the parameters estimated, the final form of the model can be given $GM(1, 1)$:

$$\hat{u}_{ij}^{(k)}(\vartheta + 1) = \left(1 - e^{a_{ij}^{(k)}}\right)\left[u_{ij}^{(k)}(1) - \frac{b_{ij}^{(k)}}{a_{ij}^{(k)}}\right] \cdot e^{-a_{ij}^{(k)}\vartheta}$$

Step 3 With the estimated grey forecasting models at your disposal, determine the optimal decision situations for the current state $s_{i_0 j_0}$ and the projected state $s_{\hat{i}_o \hat{i}_o}$. The determination of these states depends on how the decision criterion is valued and is shown in detail for the current state in Table 2.2.

Table 2.2 Selection of the optimal decision making situation for the status quo

Criterion type	Optimal decision-making situation
Maximanta (The higher the effect value, the better)	$s_{io\,jo} \Leftrightarrow \max\left(-a_{ij}^{(k)}\right) = -a_{io\,jo}^{(k)}$ $1 \le i \le n; 1 \le i \le n$
Minimanta (The smaller the effect value is, the better)	$s_{io\,jo} \Leftrightarrow \min\left(-a_{ij}^{(k)}\right) = -a_{io\,jo}^{(k)}$ $1 \le i \le n; 1 \le i \le n$
Optimanta (The closer to a moderate value, the effect is better)	$s_{io\,jo} \Leftrightarrow \min\left(\left[\frac{1}{m+n}\sum_{j=1}^{m}\sum_{i=1}^{n} a_{ij}^{(k)}\right] - a_{ij}^{(k)}\right) =$ $\left[\frac{1}{m+n}\sum_{j=1}^{m}\sum_{i=1}^{n} a_{ij}^{(k)}\right] - a_{io\,jo}^{(k)}$ $1 \le i \le n; 1 \le i \le n$

Table 2.3 Selection of the optimal decision-making situation for the forecast state

Criterion type	Optimal decision-making situation
Maximanta (The higher the effect value, the better)	$s_{\hat{i}_o\hat{i}_o} \Leftrightarrow \max(\hat{u}_{ij}^{(k)}(\vartheta+1)) = \hat{u}_{\hat{i}_o\hat{i}_o}^{(k)}(\vartheta+1)$ $1 \le i \le n;\ 1 \le i \le n$
Minimanta (The smaller the effect value is, the better)	$s_{\hat{i}_o\hat{i}_o} \Leftrightarrow \min(\hat{u}_{ij}^{(k)}(\vartheta+1)) = \hat{u}_{\hat{i}_o\hat{i}_o}^{(k)}(\vartheta+1)$ $1 \le i \le n;\ 1 \le i \le n$
Optimanta (The closer to a moderate value, the effect is better)	$s_{\hat{i}_o\hat{i}_o} \Leftrightarrow \min\left(\hat{u}_{ij}^{(k)}(\vartheta+h) - \left[\frac{1}{m+n}\sum_{j=1}^{m}\sum_{i=1}^{n}\hat{u}_{ij}^{(k)}(\vartheta+h)\right]\right) =$ $\hat{u}_{\hat{i}_o\hat{i}_o}^{(k)}(\vartheta+h) - \left[\frac{1}{m+n}\sum_{j=1}^{m}\sum_{i=1}^{n}\hat{u}_{ij}^{(k)}(\vartheta+h)\right]$ $1 \le i \le n;\ 1 \le i \le n$

Similarly, for the forecast state, Table 2.3 shows how the optimum situation is determined.

Step 4 A qualitative expert analysis should be carried out on the basis of the projected and current optimum situations. The aim is to describe the mechanisms of the analysed problem and system, as well as the environment in which the problem occurs. This knowledge will only be the basis for the decision-maker's reflections on pro-development decision patterns. This stage can be formalised, but given the methodological status of forecasting in the social sciences, further mathematical treatments will not affect the quality and reliability of the decision-making process.

The model presented requires the decision situation to be defined in a precise analytical manner. In addition, it is also necessary to define the set of criteria against which the process of selecting the optimal decision situation will be considered. In addition to the quantitative aspect, the model includes a qualitative aspect. It must be validated with qualitative expert knowledge. An important element of this model is that it allows one to look at the decision problem separately from the current state of knowledge in favour of knowledge resulting from reflection on the future.

In the group of methods designed for the administrative decision maker, the Grey Cluster Decision is a representative model. It is based on the use of a whitening function and a set of decision criteria to group the options into decision groups. Decision groups should be ordered by some valuation criterion similar to the Grey Statistical Decision model. These models are formally similar to each other. The only difference is that the evaluation of the objects is carried out analytically and in detail across predefined criteria. The model can be reduced to the following few steps [7], p. 247; [3], pp. 347–348, [56], pp. 35–36:

Step 1 Identify the number of n of decision options and m decision criteria, as well as the number of classes s, into which the individual options will be classified. The number of decision criteria and decision classes depends on the specific decision situation.

Step 2 Assign for each criterion a whitening function $f_j^k(x_{ij})$, where: x_{ij} denotes the value of the criterion in question j for $i-$ this decision variant, where: $i = 1, 2, \ldots, n$; $j = 1, 2, \ldots, m$

Step 3 Determine the importance for each decision criterion η_i in such a way that $\sum_{j=1}^{m} \eta_i$ For a larger number of criteria, consider dispensing with this step, as most methods of determining importance tend to average out and dilute the importance of the criteria, especially when they need to add up to unity.

Step 4 Determination of decision coefficients and determination of the decision vector according to the formulae:

$$\sigma_i^k = \sum_{j=1}^{m} f_j^k(x_{ij}) \cdot \eta_i$$

$$\sigma_i = (\sigma_i^1, \sigma_i^2, \ldots, \sigma_i^s)$$

Step 5 Classify the decision options into different classes. This is done in such a way that if $\max(\sigma_i^k) = \sigma_i^{k*}$, then the given decision-making variant i belongs to k^*- this decision class. However, within a decision class, several variants may be classified. The principle is that the higher the value σ_i^{k*} for a given variant, the higher the degree of membership in the class, or, in other words, the higher the rating of the variant within the class.

Grey Cluster Decision is a model that, by means of decision clusters, allows the decision space to be narrowed down to several options. In this way, it allows the professional decision-maker to identify potential directions for further analysis. Given that, in principle, a scientific approach using GST should address the problem of triangulation, it seems reasonable that the model should also be qualitatively validated.

The decision-making models presented are representative and recommended for use for particular groups of decision-makers. However, they are often modified and combined with each other [3], pp. 358–366. In addition, some models such as the Grey Incidence Decision [57], Grey Entropy and Grey Target Decision Making [58],

Dynamic Grey Target Decision Making Method [59] or Multittribute Intelligent Grey Target Decision Model [23] together with models derived from Grey Target Decision [60–62] are difficult to uniquely categorise into any group in terms of the decision-maker fit criterion. Another important problem is the frequent use of decision models in an evaluative context in the literature [63, 64], pp. 45–66, [65, 66], [7] , [67, 68]. Evaluation models consider the valuation of given objects or options to solve a problem as the main objective. The main idea of an evaluation model is to classify a selected piece of reality in terms of the needs and value structure of the evaluator. Therefore, evaluation has a cognitive dimension. It can, of course, support the decision-making process, but it does not model it. Decision models, on the other hand, try to reflect the context of the decision-making situation and are orientated in their very structure towards the causal and pragmatic aspect of the action of the subject of the decision-making process. Decision models, therefore, will definitely be more applicable to solving real-world problems of a practical nature, whereas evaluation models should be applied more appropriately to scientific and research activities. However, it should be emphasised that in a formal sense these models are similar to each other. Only the interpretation of the mathematical formalism of a given model and its context of use determine its decision-making or evaluative character.

References

1. Nowak, M., Mierzwiak, R., Pawlowska, M.: A new approach to comparison and sorting of grey numbers. In K.S. Soliman, ed. Business Excellence and Innovation Management: A 2025 Vision to Sustain Economic Development in the Era of Pandemic. no place:Proceedings of the 39th International Business Information Management Association Conference (IBIMA), pp. 1566–1577 (2022)
2. Su, W.-H., Jiang, Y.U.M.: Some opinion about two problems in the comprehensive evaluation method of grey systems. Statist. Res. **19**, 49 (2002)
3. Liu, S. and Lin, Y., 2006. *grey information: theory and practical applications.* no place:Springer Science & Business Media.
4. Liu, S., Zhang, H., Yang, Y.: Explanation of terms of grey incidence analysis models. Grey Syst. Theory Appl. (2017)
5. Liu, S., Fang, Z., Forrest, J.: On algorithm rules of interval grey numbers based on the "Kernel" and the degree of greyness of grey numbers. IEEE International Conference on Systems, Man and Cybernetics, Istanbul, IEEE, pp. 756–760 (2010)
6. Liu, S., Fang, Z., Yang, Y., Forrest, J.: General grey numbers and their operations. Grey Syst. Theory Appl. **2**, 341–349 (2012)
7. Liu, S., Yang, Y., Forrest, J.: Grey data analysis. Berlin: Springer (2017)
8. Mierzwiak, R., Nowak, M., Xie, N.: A new approach to the degree of greyness. Grey Syst. Theory Appl. **11**(2), 241–252 (2021)
9. Asad, M.M., Mohammadi, V., Shirani, M.: Modeling flexibility capabilities of IT-based supply chain, using a grey-based DEMATEL Method. Proc. Econ. Fin. **36**, 220–231 (2016)
10. Oztaysi, B.: A decision model for information technology selection using AHP integrated TOPSIS-Grey: the case of content management systems. Knowl.-Based Syst. **70**, 44–54 (2014)
11. Duleba, S., Çelikbilek, Y., Moslem, S., Esztergár-Kiss, D.: Application of grey analytic hierarchy process to estimate mode choice alternatives: a case study from Budapest. Transp. Res. Interdiscipl. Perspec. **13**, 100560 (2022)

12. Mahmoudi, A., Javed, S.A., Zhang, Z., Deng, X.: The Grey Group QUALIFLEX Method: application in Project Management. Dalian, International Conference on Intelligent System and Knowledge Engineering, ISKE (2019)
13. Fang, Z., Liu, S., Shi, H., Lin, Y.: Grey game theory and its applications in economic decision-making. Auerbach Publications, Boca Raton, London, New York (2016)
14. Jian, L., Liu, S., Lin, Y.: Hybrid rough sets and applications in uncertain decision-making. Auerbach Publications, Boca Raton, London, New York (2010)
15. Zakeri, S., Keramati, M.A.: Systematic combination of fuzzy and grey numbers for supplier selection problem. Grey Syst. Theory Appl. (2015)
16. Zanon, L.G., Carpinetti, L.C.R.: Fuzzy cognitive maps and grey systems theory in the supply chain management context: a literature review and a research proposal. no space, no name, pp. 1–8 (2018)
17. Hajek, P., Froelich, W., Prochazka, O.: Intuitionistic fuzzy grey cognitive maps for forecasting interval-valued time series. Neurocomputing **400**, 173–185 (2020)
18. Zanon, L.G.: The relationship between supply chain performance and organizational culture: a fuzzy grey cognitive maps based decision model, no place: no last name (2020)
19. Salmeron, J.L.: Modelling grey uncertainty with fuzzy grey cognitive maps. Expert Syst. Appl. **37**, 7581–7588 (2010)
20. Xie, N., Pearman, A.D.: Comparing grey number weights under interval probability information background. J. Grey Syst. **27**, 21–38 (2015)
21. Xie, N.: On computational algorithms of grey numbers based on information background. Grey Syst. Theory Appl. **3**, 177–190 (2013)
22. Liu, S., Lin, Y.: A new deflnition on degree of greyness of grey numbers with several theorems. Tuscon, IEEE Networking, Sensing and Control (2005)
23. Liu, S.: Multi-attribute intelligent grey target decision model. Taipei Taiwan, ISTASC'10: Proceedings of the 10th WSEAS international conference on systems theory and scientific computation, pp. 15–16 (2010)
24. Kuo, T.: A review of some modified grey relational analysis models. J. Grey Syst. **29**, 70–78 (2017)
25. Liu, S., Cai, H., Yang, Y.J., Cao, Y.: Advances in grey incidence analysis modelling. Syst. Eng. Theory Pract. **33**, 2041–2046 (2013)
26. Deng, J.L.: Grey system control. Huazhong University of Science and Technology Press, Wuhan (1985)
27. Liu, S., Guo, T.B.: Grey systems theory and applications. Henan University Press, Kaifeng (1991)
28. Cempel, C.: Grey systems theory-new methodology of analysis and evaluation of complex systems. J. Poznan Univers. Technol. Organiz. Manag. **63**, 9–20 (2020)
29. Deng, J.L.: Grey dynamic model and its application in the long-term forecasting output of grain (in Chinese). Disc. Nat. **3**, 37–45 (1984)
30. Xie, N., Wang, R.: A historical review of grey forecasting models. J. Grey Syst. **29** (2017)
31. Xie, N., Liu, S.: Interval grey number sequence prediction by using non-homogeneous exponential discrete grey forecasting model. J. Syst. Eng. Electr. **26**(2), 96–102 (2015)
32. Zeng, B., Liu, S., Xie, N.: Prediction model of interval grey number based on DGM (1, 1). J. Syst. Eng. Electron. **21**, 598–603 (2010)
33. Ikram, M., Zhang, Q., Sroufe, R.: Future of quality management system (ISO 9001) certification: novel grey forecasting approach. Total Qual. Manag. Bus. Excell. **32**, 1666–1693 (2021)
34. Xuemei, L. et al.: A summary of grey forecasting and relational models and its applications in marine economics and management. Marine economics and management (2019)
35. Nowak, M., Mierzwiak, R., Wojciechowski, H., Delcea, C.: Grey portfolio analysis method. Grey Syst. Theory Appl. **10**, 439–454 (2020)
36. Wu, S.-L., Zhu, J.-X., Wu, Y.-D.: Research and Application of Intelligent System of Cost Control and Profit Forecast. IERI Procedia **2**, 406–413 (2012)

37. Fergnani, A.: Corporate foresight: a new frontier for strategy and management. Acad. Manag. Persp. **36**(5), 820–844 (2022)
38. Marinković, M., Al-Tabbaa, O., Khan, Z., Wu, J.: Corporate foresight: a systematic literature review and future research trajectories. J. Busin. Res. **144**(5), 289–311 (2022)
39. Wenzel, M.: Taking the future more seriously: from-corporate foresight to future-making. Acad. Manag. Perspect. **36**(5), 845–850 (2022)
40. Mantura, W.: Overview of Qualitology. Publishing House of Poznan University of Technology, Poznań (2021)
41. Mierzwiak, R.: Systemic and cybernetic approach: applications for organization research and management methodology. *Proceedings of the 36th International Business Information Management Association Conference (IBIMA), 4–5 November 2020, Granada, Spain. Sustainable Economic Development and Advancing Education Excellence in the era of Global Pandemic,* pp. 289–299 (2020)
42. Mierzwiak, R., Nowak, M.: Decision-making models in grey systems theory (in Polish). Poznań: PTE Poznań (2020)
43. Twardowski, K.: Actions and products. Comments on the border area of psychology, grammar, and logic. In: *Semiotics in Poland 1984–1969.* no place: Springer, pp. 13–27 (1979)
44. Betti, A., casimir Twardowski. In E. N. Zalta, (ed). The Stanford Encyclopedia of Philosophy. Fall 2021 ed. no place:Metaphysics Research Lab, Stanford University (2021)
45. Flaxman, P.E., Blackledge, J.T., Bond, F.W.: Acceptance and commitment therapy: Distinctive features. Routledge, New York (2010)
46. Nowak, M., Ziomek, J.: Intuitive and rational cognition in the theory and practice of management sciences. Problemy Zarządzania, **2/2019**(5), 142–154 (2019)
47. Jain, V.: Management: Using intuition as a brain skill. South Asian Journal of Marketing & Management Research **11**, 156–162 (2021)
48. Julmi, C.: Intuition, equivocality and decision making effectiveness. Acad. Manag. Proc. **2022**(1), 10255 (2022)
49. Svenson, F., Steffen, B., Harteis, C., Launer, M.A.: Before virtuous practice. Public and Private Sector-Specific Preferences for Intuition and Deliberation in Decision-Making. Public Integrity, pp. 1–13 (2022)
50. Akinci, C., Sadler-Smith, E.: Intuition in management research: A historical review. Int. J. Manag. Rev. **14**, 104–122 (2012)
51. Mierzwiak, R., Xie, N., Dong, W.: Classification of research problems in grey system theory based on grey space concept. J. Grey Syst. **31** (2019)
52. Gao, W.: Grey Statistical Decision Making for Estimate of the Regional Wheat Trials Yield. Atlantis Press, Xi'an (2018)
53. Kung, C.-Y., Yan, T.-M., Huang, C.-C.: Using grey statistic method to evaluate the optimal distribution for strategic resources in medium and small enterprise. Singapore, 2008 IEEE International Conference on Systems, Man and Cybernetics, pp. 2866–2871 (2008)
54. Tai, Y.-Y., Lin, J.-Y., Chen, M.-S., Lin, M.-C.: A grey decision and prediction model for investment in the core competitiveness of product development. Technol. Forecast. Soc. Change **78**(9), 1254–1267 (2011)
55. Zhang, C., Cao, J.: A dynamic resource management strategy for cloud based on sequential decision model and demand forecast. Beijing , IEEE International Conference on Cloud and Service Computing (2013)
56. Golinska, P., Kosacka, M., Mierzwiak, R., Werner-Lewandowska, K.: Grey decision making as a tool for the classification of the sustainability level of remanufacturing companies. J. Clean. Prod. **105**, 28–40 (2015)
57. Jian, L., Dixin, L., Dang, L.: Research on grey incidence decision-making with uncertainty. Nanjing , IEEE, pp. 1077–1081 (2008)
58. Julong, D.: Grey entropy and grey target decision making. J. Grey Syst. **22**, 1–4 (2010)
59. Yan, S., Liu, S., Liu, X.: Dynamic grey target decision making method with three-parameter grey numbers. Leicester, IEEE International Conference on Grey Systems and Intelligent Services (GSIS), pp. 346–351 (2015)

60. Yaoguo, D., Sifeng, L., Bin, L.: On the multi-attribute weighted grey target decision. no place, no name, pp. 796–798 (2004)
61. Ruan, A., Wang, Y.: The multiple attribute decision model of grey targets based on grey potential degree. Grey Syst. Theory Appl. **7**, 365–375 (2017)
62. Ruan, A., Yin, X., Chen, Q., Wang, Y.: Standard grey potential and its application in grey target decision. no place, no name, pp. 437–441 (2016)
63. Liu, S., Xie, N., Forrest, J.: Novel models of grey relational analysis based on visual angle of similarity and nearness. Grey Syst. Theory Appl. **1**(1), 8–18 (2011)
64. Liu, S., Xie, N., Yuan, C., Fang, Z.: Systems evaluation: methods, models, and applications. Boca Raton, London , New York: CRC Press (2011)
65. Cao, B., Liu, Y., Qian, W.-Y., Wang, Y.-H.: Construction of the evaluation system for regional road traffic safety and application based on a grey integrated evaluation model. Leicester, IEEE International Conference on Grey Systems and Intelligent Services (GSIS), pp. 395–403 (2015)
66. Liu, S., et al.: Research on index system for disabled elders evaluation and grey clustering model based on end-point mixed possibility functions. J. Grey Syst. **31**(4), 1–12 (2019)
67. Luo, H., Lin, X.: Application of the grey comprehensive evaluation in the project bid evaluation. no place, no name, pp. 609–612 ((2010))
68. Zheng, W., Hu, Y.: Grey evaluation method of knowledge management capability. no space, IEEE (2009)
69. Xie, N, Liu, S.-f.: Novel methods on comparing grey numbers. Appl. Mathem. Model., **34**(2), 415–423 (2010)
70. Deng, J.: Grey control system. Printing House of Central China University of Science and Technology, Hubei. (1985)

Chapter 3
The Use of Grey Systems Theory Methods in Management Sciences in Literature Research

3.1 The Literature Research Methodology

The theoretical analysis in the previous chapters has identified potential directions for the application of grey methods in management science research. However, it is important to identify the current state of research in this area and to publish it in the literature. Therefore, it is advisable to conduct a systematic analysis of the literature. The main aim of this analysis is to answer the following research questions:

- In which substantive areas in management science research are grey systems theory methods applicable?
- What is the place of methods of grey systems theory in the structure of research conducted in management science?
- What is the rationale for using grey methods in research in management science?
- With which methods and analytical approaches are grey systems theory methods combined?

In the first step of the systematic literature review to answer the identified research questions, the objective was to collect an initial database of literature sources related to the topic of the review. For this purpose, the databases of the Scopus and Web of Science literature were searched. The databases of the literature were used in such a way that abstracts and titles were searched for keywords. Furthermore, it was assumed that only scientific articles would be included in the analysis, with the exclusion of book chapters or post-conference articles. Furthermore, the scope of the search was narrowed down to areas directly or indirectly related to the management sciences. For this purpose, the set of classification categories available in the databases searched was used. This was extremely important due to the fact that often some keywords are used in different contexts that may not be related to management science or grey systems theory. The key words related to grey systems theory were grey, system, relational, number, forecast, decision, and evaluation. These are linked to the main methods of grey systems theory and were combined with further keywords such as

R. Mierzwiak, *Methodological Aspects of Grey Systems Theory in Management Research*, Series on Grey System, https://doi.org/10.1007/978-981-97-2413-0_3

management and business. The detailed query structure of the databases searched is shown in Table 3.1.

A search of the Web of Science and Scopus databases using the queries shown in Table 3.1 and combining them into one database yielded 201 items from the literature. In the next step, duplicates were automatically removed using the JabRef literature manager. As a result, the size of the database was reduced to 91 items. In the next step, the title and abstracts were analysed, and thus reduced the size of the database to 45 items. They were subjected to a thorough content analysis and 6 items were excluded. The excluded items together with the reasons for exclusion are shown in Table 3.2.

The criteria for excluding the items in the literature in question from the further study were, in two cases, that the items were classified as economics, not management issues [2, 3]. A distinction was made between publications in these two disciplines in that if the problematic nature of the publication concerned issues of analysis of the industry as a whole and was not managerial in nature, such a publication was classified into economics and excluded from further analysis. The managerial nature of the publication was determined in the context of the research results that it presented. If the results of the research could assist individual managerial decisions more than the regulatory and policy activities of public institutions, it was considered to meet the criteria for inclusion of the research as relevant to management science. In one case, an item that was a chapter in a monograph was excluded [1]. The adoption of such a criterion is due to the fact that often in monographs the research is illustrative and conceptual in nature. In some cases, it is also difficult to identify information on the quality of the review process.

Another exclusion criterion for one case was that the publication was a review. The item was a literature review and was not a typical empirical paper [4]. Therefore,

Table 3.1 Structure of queries to literature databases

L.p	Keywords	Base name	
		Scopus	Web of science
1	"Grey system" and ("Management" or "Business")	27	14
2	"Grey relational" and ("Management" or "Business")	14	11
3	"Grey decision" and ("Management" or "Business")	36	30
4	"Grey forecast" and ("Management" or "Business")	4	2
5	"Grey number" and ("Management" or "Business")	15	6
6	"Grey evaluation" and ("Management" or "Business")	25	17
Total publication		121	80

Table 3.2 Items excluded from the literature survey

Title	Authors	Reasons for exclusion
Improving the E-store business model for satisfying customers' needs using a hybrid MCDM combined DANP with grey relational model	Chiu et al. [1]	The publication is a chapter of the monograph
Reconfiguring the innovation policy portfolios for Taiwan's SIP Mall industry	Huang et al. [2]	The publication deals with issues related to the problems of economics
Optimising factors for the accuracy of forecasting models in food processing industry: a context of cacao manufacturers in Vietnam	Nguyen [3]	The publication deals with issues related to the problems of economics
Supply chain management during and post-COVID-19 pandemic: mitigation strategies and practical lessons learned	Raj et al. [4]	The publication is a review of the literature
Evaluation of robustness of supply chain information sharing strategies using a hybrid Taguchi and multiple-criteria decision-making method	Yang et al. [5]	The text does not use grey systems theory methods in the research process
Key success factors of holding exhibitions for the exhibition organizers using dramaturgy model and grey relational analysis	Pan et al. [6]	The publication does not explain the research method in a precise way. It does not clearly show the position of the GRA in the structure of the research process

it could not be included in further analyses due to the fact that the purpose of the literature review conducted is to identify the current state of GST applications in research processes conducted in management sciences.

In addition, one publication only mentioned grey systems theory; however, it was not applicable to the research process [5]. Therefore, this item was not included in future considerations. However, in another case, the methodological structure of the article was unclear [6]. There was a lack of clearly defined research steps. The grey relationship analysis method was described in a theoretical way; however, it was difficult to clearly identify its importance in the overall research process. Research results were also presented in an abbreviated manner. The operations conducted on the empirical data were not clearly shown. Therefore, due to these arguments, the article was excluded from further analysis.

An overview of the literature research process is shown in Fig. 3.1. This diagram is based on the PRISMA 2009 model.

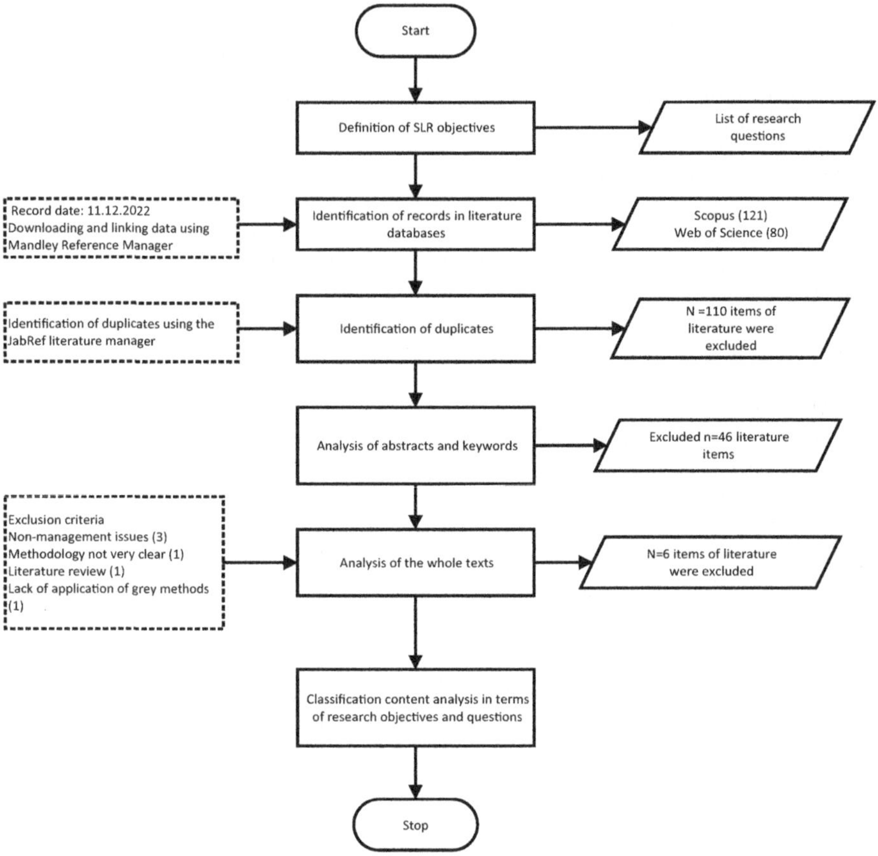

Fig. 3.1 A systematic literature review process based on the PRISMA model

3.2 Thematical Area of GST Management Applications

As a result of the selection of publications, the number of texts analysed was limited and 39 items of literature were analysed. The main element of the analysis was the identification of the research results achieved and a preliminary indication of the research area. The collected results are shown in Table 3.3. The sorting key was the author's name.

To better classify the content of the publications analysed, Table 3.4 classifies them into the following thematic groups: logistics management, business process management, production management and engineering, environmental management, strategic management, knowledge management.

The area of management issues in which GST methods have been most frequently used is that of logistics management and, in particular, supply chain management issues. Research in this area has often been combined with sustainability and the

Table 3.3 GST in management science by topic

Title	Authors	Results/area of research
Remanufacturing supply chain: an analysis of performance indicator areas	Ansari et al. [7]	Key factors influencing the efficiency of the remanufacturing supply chain business processes were identified
A grey-based DEMATEL model for evaluating business process management critical success factors	Bai and Sarkis [8]	Factors influencing the efficiency of BPM (business process management) practices were identified and classified
Evaluating ecological sustainable performance measures for supply chain management	Bai et al. [9]	A model for assessing and monitoring performance in sustainable supply chains has been developed
Analyzing organizational barriers towards building post-pandemic supply chain resilience in Indian MSMEs: a grey-DEMATEL approach	Banerjee [10]	Barriers affecting the resilience of supply chains were identified and the relationships between these barriers were explored for small and medium-sized enterprises in India. These barriers were identified at the tactical and operational levels
Multi-approach model for selection of SCMS in semiconductor industry upstream	Chang et al. [11]	A hierarchical and structural supply chain assessment model was developed and validated using the semiconductor industry as an example
Exploring critical factors of green business failure based on Grey-Decision Making Trial and Evaluation Laboratory (DEMATEL)	Cui et al. [12]	A set of critical factors and the relationships between them that affect the success of businesses targeting the green business area were identified
Fostering reverse logistics in India by prominent barrier identification and strategy implementation to promote circular economy	Dutta et al. [13]	Significant barriers are identified affecting the implementation of the concept of reverse logistics and a set of business strategies to implement clean production principles is proposed
Analyzing the risks of adopting circular economy initiatives in manufacturing supply chains	Ethirajan et al. [14]	The relationship between factors affecting the implementation of circular economy initiatives in supply chains was analysed, and a set of business strategies to minimise risks in the implementation of such initiatives was developed
Benchmark the best factory data collection system (FDC) using AHP-GRA method	Gangurde [15]	A method was developed to select a Factory Data Collection (FDC) system. Then, using this method, a case study was shown where the best solution was selected from the set of solutions obtained through the benchmarking process

(continued)

Table 3.3 (continued)

Title	Authors	Results/area of research
Analyzing the impact of COVID-19 on the financial performance of the hospitality and tourism industries: an ensemble MCDM approach in the Indian context	Ghosh and Bhattacharya [16]	A model was developed to assess the economic performance of players in the tourism industry and the impact of the pandemic crisis on their business operations was examined through this model
An integrated model for supplier selection: an automobile industry case study	Gnanasekaran et al. [17]	A decision model for supplier selection was developed. The model was verified using an example from the automotive industry
Structural model for analysis of key performance indicators for sustainable manufacturer-supplier collaboration: a grey-decision-making trial and evaluation laboratory-based approach	Govindan et al. [18]	Key success factors have been identified for supplier assessment. These factors can form the basis for monitoring sustainable supply chain collaboration
Towards agility in international high-tech SMEs: exploring key drivers and main outcomes of dynamic capabilities	Jafari-Sadeghi et al. [19]	A set of factors and relationships between them that affect the agility of small and medium-sized technology companies in international markets were identified
An integer grey goal programming for project time, cost, and quality trade-offs	Hajiagha et al. [20]	A model based on graph theory was developed to optimise project management decisions in the context of time, cost, and quality trade-off issues
Barriers in implementing lean manufacturing in Indian SMEs: a multi-criteria decision-making approach	Jaiswal et al. [21]	Factors and relationships between them related to barriers to the implementation of lean manufacturing in small and medium enterprises were identified
The new concept of quality in the digital era: a human resource empowerment perspective	Jamkhaneh et al. [22]	A set of factors affecting the quality of human resources was identified in relation to the requirements of the Industry 4.0 concept
Enablers to implement circular initiatives in the supply chain: a grey DEMATEL method	Khan et al. [23]	The factors and relationships between them that are activators of circular economy initiatives implemented in organisations were identified and assessed

(continued)

Table 3.3 (continued)

Title	Authors	Results/area of research
Transition management theory-based policy framework for analysing environmentally responsible freight transport practices	Kumar [24]	A classification of a set of practices related to environmentally responsible transport practices was made. The model was validated using a case study example in the freight transport industry
Industry 4.0 as an enabler of sustainability diffusion in supply chain: an analysis of influential strength of drivers in an emerging economy	Luthra et al. [25]	The aim of the article is to investigate key drivers of Industry 4.0 to diffuse sustainability in Supply Chains (SCs) from the perspective of an emerging economy and to analyse the influential strength (cause-effect interrelationship) of listed key drivers
What drives inter-organisational knowledge management? The cause and effect analysis using a multi-layer multi-criteria decision-making framework	Mahdiraji et al. [26]	The article aimed to identify and assess the network of factors influencing knowledge management in inter-organisational arrangements
Performance evalution in strategic alliances: a case of Vietnamese construction industry	Nguyen [27]	The paper demonstrates a method for investigating the potential to enter strategic alliances with manufacturing companies. The method was verified using a case study example in the construction industry
A 3-dimensional frame of reference for prevention of risk in supply chain	Nguyen [28]	The article identifies a set of factors that can help managers avoid risk in supply chains. The research was carried out in supermarket chains
Using optimization algorithms of DEA and grey system theory in strategic partner selection: an empirical study in Vietnam steel industry	Nguyen and Nguyen [29]	The text shows a model for supplier selection and evaluation based on performance analysis and predictive data
A study of the strategic alliance for Vietnam domestic pharmaceutical industry: a dynamic integration of a hybrid DEA and GM (1,1) approach	Nguyen and Tran [30]	The article shows an efficiency model and a dynamic time model for assessing the potential of pharmaceutical companies

(continued)

Table 3.3 (continued)

Title	Authors	Results/area of research
Using a hybrid decision-making model to evaluate the sustainable development performance of high-tech listed companies	Ou [31]	A model was developed and verified to assess organisational sustainability using selected high tech companies as an example
Supply chain recovery challenges in the wake of COVID-19 pandemic	Raj et al. [4]	Factors and relationships between them that affect the reconstruction of disrupted supply chains in the garment industry were identified
Supplier selection using combined AHP and GRA for a pump manufacturing industry	Sandeep et al. [32]	A hybrid supplier selection model was developed. The model was verified using the example of a company that produces centrifugal and submersible pumps
An integrated GRA-DEMATEL-ANP framework for evaluation of barriers to implementation of green supply chain management in manufacturing industries	Sangari et al. [33]	Barriers affecting the implementation of the green supply chain management concept in automotive companies were identified
Applications of information and communication technology for sustainable growth of SMEs in India food industry	Singh et al. [34]	The key factors influencing the adoption of ICT in the food industry in the context of sustainability issues were identified
An integrated Grey-DEMATEL approach for evaluating ICT adoption barriers in manufacturing SMEs analyzing Indian MSMEs	Singh et al. [35]	An expert model was developed to identify barriers related to ICT adoption in small and medium enterprises
Combining AHP and GRA model for evaluation property-liability insurance companies to rank	Tsai et al. [36]	A hierarchical and multifaceted performance evaluation model was developed for companies in the insurance industry

(continued)

Table 3.3 (continued)

Title	Authors	Results/area of research
Assessment on intellectual capital management for Taiwanese pharmaceutical industry: using GRA and MPI	Wang et al. [37]	A relational model was developed to assess the effectiveness of intellectual capital use in pharmaceutical companies
Foreign markets expansion for air medical transport business	Wang et al. [38]	A hierarchical model has been developed to assess the potential of a given foreign market. The model helps managers make decisions about expansion into a given foreign market. The model was verified for the private medical transport market
Evaluating business performance of wealth management banks	Wu et al. [39]	Developed multi-criteria model for assessing bank performance, operationalising the balanced scorecard concept
Green marketing: a grey-based rough set theory analysis of activities	Xu et al. [40]	A set of activities related to the concept of green marketing was identified and evaluated. The research was conducted in terms of its relevance to supply chain management
Contextual and organisational factors in sustainable supply chain decision making: grey relational analysis and interpretative structural modelling	Yang et al. [41]	This paper identifies a set of factors and the relationships between them that affect sustainable supply chain management. The research was carried out in Chinese manufacturing companies
Adopting information systems for china enterprise investing using the grey relation analysis	Yuan and Chen [42]	A multifaceted model for the implementation of information systems in companies was developed and validated
Barriers to environmentally-friendly clothing production among Chinese apparel companies	Zhu et al. [43]	Barriers to the implementation of green solutions in garment companies were identified in network terms

(continued)

Table 3.3 (continued)

Title	Authors	Results/area of research
Decision making on advertising strategy selection based on life cycle of products by applying FAHP and	Zolfani et al. [44]	A multicriteria model was developed to evaluate the different advertising channels. The model allows individual channels to be classified against a set of adopted criteria
TOPSIS Grey: growth stage perspective; a case about food industry in Iran	Zolfani et al. [45]	In this paper, hybrid MCDM methods applied to select advertising strategy considering the product life cycle of products. The results of this research illustrated that monthly cost, content and educational level are three important criteria in advertising strategy and also newspaper is the best way for advertising and after that television is next and radio, environmental advertising, and Internet and SMS are after those in this case in growth step of product life cycle

circular economy. In the proposed classification, articles related to sustainability and ecology in management in the broadest sense were grouped under the category: environmental management. Furthermore, in the field of logistics management, GST methods were also used in the context of a classic problem in supply chains, namely the modelling of decision-making processes related to supplier selection. In addition to logistics-related issues, GST methods were also used in the context of strategic management. In this group, studies addressing problems related to the operationalisation and measurement of the performance of adopted organisational and design solutions of strategic nature were classified. In the category of process management, articles were classified which, on the one hand, described classic issues in this area, such as modelling with the use of BPM, and, on the other hand, issues related to the improvement of business processes with the use of ICT technologies. In the category of production management and engineering, articles were classified that deal with issues in the area of lean manufacturing, production efficiency and the Industry 4.0 concept, while in the category of knowledge management, articles related to the quality of human resources and intellectual capital formation processes were classified, with particular emphasis on the opportunities, threats, and barriers resulting from the increasing adoption of ICT technologies in modern organisations.

Table 3.4 Classification of subject matter of articles that integrate GST methods with management research

Authors of the article/ year	Logistics management	Business process management	Production management and engineering	Environmental management	Strategic management	Knowledge management
Ansari et al. [7]	√			√		
Bai and Sarkis [8]		√				
Bai et al. [9]	√			√		
Banerjee et al. [10]	√					
Chang et al. [11]	√					
Cui et al. [12]				√	√	
Dutta et al. [13]						
Ethirajan et al. [14]	√		√	√		
Gangurde [15]	√			√		
Ghosh and Bhattacharya [16]					√	
Gnanasekaran et al. [17]	√					
Govindan et al. [18]	√					
Jafari-Sadeghi et al. [19]			√			

(continued)

Table 3.4 (continued)

Authors of the article/year	Logistics management	Business process management	Production management and engineering	Environmental management	Strategic management	Knowledge management
Hajiagha et al. [20]					√	
Jaiswal et al. [21]			√			
Jamkhaneh et al. [22]			√			
Khan et al. [23]	√			√		
Kumar [24]	√			√		
Luthra et al. [25]	√		√			
Mahdiraji et al. [26]						√
Nguyen [27]					√	
Nguyen [28]	√					
Nguyen and Nguyen [29]	√					
Nguyen and Tran [30]					√	
Ou [31]					√	
Raj et al. [4]	√					
Sandeep et al. [32]	√					
Sangari et al. [33]	√			√		
Singh et al. [34]		√				√
Singh et al. [35]		√				√
Tsai et al. [36]					√	

(continued)

Table 3.4 (continued)

Authors of the article/year	Logistics management	Business process management	Production management and engineering	Environmental management	Strategic management	Knowledge management
Wang et al. [37]						√
Wang et al. [38]					√	
Wu et al. [39]					√	
Xu et al. [40]	√			√		
Yang et al. [41]	√			√		
Yuan and Chen [42]		√				
Zhu et al. [43]				√		
Zolfani et al. [44]					√	

3.3 Rationale for the Application of the Grey Systems Theory to Management Science Research

Grey systems theory is an analytical approach that in many applications is an alternative to statistical modelling, fuzzy logic, or rough set theory. The default approach in quantitative research in the management sciences is statistical analysis of results. This is because the dominant research paradigm in contemporary management science is the neopositivist-functionalist-systems (NFS) paradigm. It assumes that knowledge should be best obtained in representative research procedures with high-quality research samples. Hence, the extensive use of statistics is natural and needs no justification. When, on the other hand, for various reasons, a representative research strategy is impossible or difficult to apply, an important element of the research is to justify the choice of another approach to the analysis of empirical data. This applies equally to the use of grey systems theory, fuzzy logic, or rough set theory. Without such a justification, the research can be regarded as more demonstrative than cognitive. To analyse the justifications for the applications of GST in management sciences, Table 3.5 synthesises these justifications on the basis of publications reviewed in depth in a systematic literature review (SLR).

An area of research in management science is complex socio-technical systems and the phenomena occurring within them. The dynamism and complexity of management issues make it difficult in many cases to describe them quantitatively. Grey systems theory can be a convenient methodology for carrying out quantification operations with relatively unrestrictive assumptions on data quality. In the analysis of the literature carried out in Table 3.5, the dominant justification for the use of grey analytical methods is their ease of application in terms of transforming scores expressed on linguistic scales into grey numbers. Such an operation is as correct as possible and, in many problems, much easier than the use of fuzzy logic, statistics, or rough set theory. However, due to the small number of works addressing the methodology of grey systems theory in the context of the specific social sciences, the justifications for the use of grey research methods in the analysed publications are insufficient. Mainly, the arguments in them refer to the grey box concept and show the genesis of GST and its general research assumptions. The argumentation of small amounts of uncertain data as the main domain of GST applications is also frequently indicated. The concept of a grey box in the justifications in the analysed publications is therefore treated metaphorically, not axiomatically. It therefore does not fully respect the rigour of a rational, logical, and deductive approach to methodology.

Table 3.5 Rationale for using grey methods in management research work

Authors	Rationale for using GST methods
Ansari et al. [7]	GST methods were used because of the ease of transforming expert linguistic judgments into grey numbers in the problem of evaluating relationships between factors in the DEMATEL (Decision Making Trial and Evaluation Laboratory) method. The advantage of GST over the fuzzy approach was pointed out. The advantage, according to the authors, was that no membership function had to be constructed
Bai and Sarkis [8]	GST methods were used because of the ease of transforming expert linguistic judgments into grey numbers in the problem of assessing relationships between factors in the DEMATEL method. The use of GST methods was justified on the grounds that they are designed for the analysis of complex and uncertain phenomena of a qualitative nature, for the quantification of which the modelling of group expert judgments is needed
Bai et al. [9]	GST methods were used in the context of building a decision-making system based on rough set theory. The argumentation for the use of the grey number approach in the evaluation of the individual criteria made a very vague reference to grey systems theory as one approach to uncertainty analysis. The argumentation is nonspecific and unconvincing. On the other hand, the article itself is demonstrative of the new method in relation to example data
Banerjee [10]	The article argues that grey system theory helps in solving problems of uncertain and incomplete information and eliminates individual biases Moreover, it was pointed out that the major advantage of using grey theory in the current study setup is that it allows a limited amount of data to be obtained under uncertainty obtained from a small sample
Chang et al. [11]	The article demonstrates a new method for evaluating and selecting suppliers. The findings are based on a case study example. The justification for the use of GRA in prioritising evaluation criteria is at a high level of generality. The justification is unconvincing and nonexhaustive
Cui et al. [12]	GST methods were used because of the ease of transformation of expert linguistic evaluations into grey numbers in the problem of evaluating relationships between factors in the DEMATEL method. It was argued that grey analytical methods easily allow for the numerical expression of qualitative criteria in expert-led evaluation. Furthermore, in general, it was argued that the main domain of GST is the analysis of uncertain data generated by complex social systems
Dutta et al. [13]	GST methods were used because of the ease of transforming expert linguistic judgments into grey numbers in the problem of assessing relationships between factors in the DEMATEL method. The use of grey numbers was justified by a general digression on the fact that GST models are adequate for uncertain data and that relatively few are needed for analysis. Furthermore, it was pointed out that the collected data can have quite a lot of variation and variability

(continued)

Table 3.5 (continued)

Authors	Rationale for using GST methods
Ethirajan et al. [14]	GST methods were used because of the ease of transforming expert linguistic judgements to grey numbers in the problem of assessing the relationships between factors in the DEMATEL method. Argumentation for the use of grey methods was based on the very general statement that GST models are the right choice when faced with complex decision problems. The argumentation is general, however, supported by a brief review of the literature in this area
Gangurde [15]	GRA relationship analysis was applied to the evaluation of the evaluation criteria. There is no justification as to why the grey approach was used in solving the problem. The article focusses on demonstrating a new methodological tool
Ghosh and Bhattacharya [16]	The GRA method was used in the context of evaluating the weighting of the different options in the decision model. The article does not provide a justification for the use of GRA. The findings are more in the nature of a case study of the application of a new methodological solution
Gnanasekaran et al. [17]	A GRA approach was used to integrate qualitative and quantitative data, considering its characteristics larger-is-better or smaller-is-better. The paper lacks a justification for the use of the grey approach in the research. Only the assumptions of relational models in grey system theory are described in general terms. The research results are more in the nature of a case study of the application of a new methodological solution
Govindan et al. [18]	GST methods were used because of the ease of transforming expert linguistic judgments into grey numbers in the problem of assessing relationships between factors in the DEMATEL method. Argumentation for using this approach was based on very general considerations related to the properties of GST methods for uncertain data. The study lacks an in-depth and comprehensive justification
Jafari-Sadeghi et al. [19]	This paper uses grey numbers to model expert judgments in the context of the DEMATEL method. However, only basic arithmetic operations on grey numbers are shown. The validity of its use has not been fully justified. Only a general argument about small-size and uncertain data as a domain of grey systems theory was referred to
Hajiagha et al. [20]	The text gives the basics of grey operations needed in linear programming to solve the time–cost-quality trade-off problem. No justification is given as to why grey numbers were used, and no rationale is given. The findings are more in the nature of a case study of the application of a new methodological solution
Jaiswal et al. [21]	GST methods were used because of the ease of transforming expert linguistic judgments into grey numbers in the problem of assessing relationships between factors in the DEMATEL method. However, a clear and convincing justification for this methodology is lacking in the article. It was only pointed out that the data from the expert assessments belong to the category of uncertain data and hence the sense of using GST methods based on grey numbers

(continued)

Table 3.5 (continued)

Authors	Rationale for using GST methods
Jamkhaneh et al. [22]	GST methods were chosen because of the ease of transformation of expert linguistic judgements to grey numbers in the problem of assessing relationships between factors in the DEMATEL method. The rationale is at a general level referring to the thesis that grey systems theory is a methodology for analysing small numbers of uncertain data
Khan et al. [23]	GST methods were used because of the ease of transforming expert linguistic judgments into grey numbers in the problem of assessing relationships between factors in the DEMATEL method. However, a clear and convincing justification for this methodology is lacking in the article. It was only pointed out that the grey approach has good effects in situations with imprecise and subjective data
Kumar [24]	GST methods were used because of the ease of transformation of expert linguistic evaluations to grey numbers in the context of the calculation procedure in the VIKOR method (Visekriterijumska Optimizacija i Kompromisno Resenje) method. The rationale behind the use of grey methods was to refer to the general criterion of being able to analyse uncertain, difficult to quantify, imprecise, and subjective data
Luthra et al. [25]	GST methods were used because of the ease of transforming expert linguistic judgments into grey numbers in the problem of assessing relationships between factors in the DEMATEL method. The use of the grey approach was not justified in any way. The method was adopted arbitrarily
Mahdiraji et al. [26]	GST methods were used because of the ease of transforming expert linguistic judgments into grey numbers in the problem of assessing relationships between factors in the DEMATEL method. The use of the grey approach was not justified in any way. The method was adopted arbitrarily
Nguyen [27]	Grey forecasting methods were used in this paper. Their justification for using them was due to the small amount of data in the time series. In such cases, it should be noted that GM models can achieve satisfactory results. The rationale is therefore correct, although a qualitative in-depth analysis of the system for which the grey forecasting model was built was not made
Nguyen [28]	The GM (1,1) predictive model was used to extend and deepen the descriptive and explanatory research. No justification was given for using the grey approach. The method was adopted arbitrarily
Nguyen and Nguyen [29]	The GM (1,1) predictive model was used to complement the Data Envelopment Analysis (DEA) study. The use of the grey approach was not justified in any way. The method was adopted arbitrarily in the research
Nguyen and Tran [30]	The predictive model GM (1,1) was used, integrating it with the DEA method. The use of the grey approach was not convincingly justified. Only the properties of grey predictive models were discussed in general terms. These models were arbitrarily adopted in the study
Ou [31]	The paper uses the GRA model in combination with the DEMATEL method. The reasoning behind the grey approach is not clearly shown. The text shows new methodological approaches on empirical data from high-tech companies

(continued)

Table 3.5 (continued)

Authors	Rationale for using GST methods
Raj et al. [4]	This paper shows the modelling of evaluation processes using quantification by grey numbers. The rationale for using the grey approach was that it allows, in a much easier way than fuzzy logic, to analyse qualitative uncertain data. It was emphasised that fuzzy logic requires the definition of a membership function, which in many cases is constructed arbitrarily. Hence, the absence of such assumptions when operating on grey numbers makes this approach more flexible and much easier computationally and interpretatively
Sandeep et al. [32]	The text applies the GRA method in the context of decision-making processes conducted using the Analytic Hierarchy Process (AHP) approach. The rationale refers to the fact that the GRA method is designed to analyse relationships in a set of uncertain, small-volume data. The work presented here is a case study and aims to demonstrate the hybrid decision-making model developed. Therefore, the rationale is given a secondary treatment
Sangari ett al. [33]	This paper integrates the DEMATEL method with the GRA approach using grey numbers and the Analytical Network Process (ANP) method. The rationale behind the use of the grey approach is that it is adequate for uncertain data derived from assessments expressed on linguistic scales
Singh et al. [34]	This paper uses grey numbers to quantify qualitative expert judgements for the DEMATEL method. The use of the grey approach was justified by the high vagueness of the data and its uncertainty and smallness
Singh et al. [35]	The text uses grey numbers to analyse expert visits in relation to the application of the DEMATEL method. The use of this approach was justified by considering the nature of grey information by referring to the cybernetic concept of black, white, and grey boxes. It was argued that the problem addressed in the paper contains grey information and requires a GST analytical approach
Tsai et al. [36]	This paper demonstrates the use of the GRA method in the construction of an evaluation model for a selected category of enterprises. This model was used because it allows for the analysis of a small number of data from expert evaluations. Furthermore, it was emphasised that this model, unlike traditional statistical methods, does not make any assumptions about the distribution of the data
Wang et al. [37]	The text shows the integration of the GRA and DEA model to assess the performance of a selected group of companies. The article does not convincingly describe the methodological aspects of using the grey approach. The research focusses more on demonstrating the capabilities of the developed evaluation model

(continued)

Table 3.5 (continued)

Authors	Rationale for using GST methods
Wang et al. [38]	This paper demonstrates the application of the AHP method using grey numbers for exploratory comparative assessments. The rationale for the use of the grey approach was argued to be adequate for uncertain data. However, no justification was given in the given application context. Only general information about grey systems theory, its general assumptions and genesis was indicated
Wu et al. [39]	The paper shows an assessment model using the AHP method and the GRA model. The GRA model was used because it does not require the data to have a specific distribution, and it was emphasised that it can be used with a relatively small amount of data
Xu et al. [40]	This paper presents a model based on rough set theory that generates decision rules from data implemented using grey numbers. The rationale for the use of the grey approach is based on general statements about the uncertainty of the data and its ability to be modelled using GST, giving a brief historical overview of the theory
Yang et al. [41]	This paper uses the GRA model, integrating it with the Interpretative Structural Modelling (ISM) method. The use of the grey approach was justified by general statements about the information generated in systems about whose structure and functioning mechanisms we have uncertain and grey knowledge
Yuan and Chen [42]	In this paper, the GRA model was applied to the ranking of criteria. The rationale for using grey methods shows their advantages over classical statistics, namely: nonparametric models, easy to calculate, no strict sample size requirement, no assumption for normal distribution of data, no paradox analysis with quantity analysis
Zhu et al. [43]	This paper shows the integration of the DEMATEL method with algebraic operations on grey numbers. The model was used to quantify expert linguistic judgements. The justification for the use of grey numbers is reduced to only a few general descriptions that present the genesis and development of practical applications of GST
Zolfani et al. [44]	This paper demonstrates a hybrid decision-making method that combines the TOPSIS method (Technique for Order Preference by Similarity to Ideal Solution) and the AHP method. In the context of the TOPSIS method, grey number arithmetic was applied to computational processes. The paper does not discuss the methodological issues involved in justifying the choice of grey modelling in decision-making processes

3.4 Ways of Integrating Grey Methods with Other Research Approaches in the Analysis of Management Problems

Grey systems theory has great potential for integration with other methods. With it, it is therefore possible to generate models of a hybrid nature. The grey approach can have a different position and importance in the structure of such models. In the first case, grey systems theory can be integrated within other methods, improving their internal analytical mechanisms. In the second case, on the other hand, systems theory models can be combined in series or in parallel with other methods, providing analysis of the original data for them or analysing the results they produce. In general, therefore, we can state that GST models can be used as.

- The information processor, i.e. the main model or analytical system through which the desired results of the research conducted are obtained;
- An information preprocessor, i.e. an analytical model or system that operates on primary data and passes the results of the analyses to the information processor;
- An information post-processor, i.e. an analytical model or system through which analyses of the results obtained from the information processor are facilitated.

Respecting the division into preprocessor, processor, and postprocessor as the elementary units of any methodological approach focused on information processing, Table 3.6 shows how grey models are positioned and integrated with other analytical methods in the management literature.

Summarising the results of the analysis of the integration of GST with other methodological solutions in the context of management science, it should be stated that:

- Grey systems theory methods are mainly used in research strategies based on expert knowledge modelling.
- The position of grey systems theory methods in the research structure in the context of management science is mainly the modelling of input data using grey numbers, thus extending the possibilities of other research methodologies.
- A particularly common way to integrate GST with other research methods is to use grey numbers and the DEMATEL method to analyse networks of factors influencing given organisational phenomena and processes.
- In an approach called grey DEMATEL, a common element to support the analysis is grey number whitening using the CFCS method and post-processing the results using the CoCoSo method.
- Grey factor analysis is often combined with decision-making methods such as AHP/ANP or SAW, where its main purpose is to support the ranking of options or decision criteria.
- Grey relationship analysis is also used in conjunction with the DEA method as a complement or triangulation to give credibility to the results.
- Grey relationship analysis, on the other hand, is incidentally associated with network analysis, mainly a rarely used version of the Grey DEMATE method or the Interpretative Structural Model method, where in both cases the input matrix is the result of preprocessing the data with GRA.
- Grey predictive models served primarily in the DEA efficiency analysis, introducing an input extrapolation component based on a small amount of historical data.
- It is a big surprise that grey decision-making and evaluation models have not found widespread use in management research, which may be due more to their utilitarian and less cognitive nature.

Table 3.6 Grey systems theory in the structure of management research processes

Article authors/ year	Position in the information analysis process			Methods used		Comments
	Preprocessor	Processor	Post-processor	GST	Other	
Ansari et al. [7]	√			Grey numbers	DEMATEL, CFCS (Converting Fuzzy Data into Crisp Scores)	In this paper, grey numbers were used to quantify the expert linguistic scales used to evaluate relationships in the agent network. In this way, the grey direct-relation matrices were generated, on which the underlying calculations were then performed using grey algebraic operations and the CFCS (converting fuzzy data into crisp scores) method modified for grey numbers
Bai and Sarkis [8]	√	√		Grey numbers	DEMATEL	The paper uses grey numbers to quantify linguistic scales and grey number arithmetic in matrix calculations in the DEMATEL method
Bai et al. [9]	√	√		Grey numbers	Rough Set	The text uses grey numbers to quantify linguistic evaluations and basic algebraic operations on grey numbers to determine neighbourhood rough sets
Banerjee et al. [10]	√	√		Grey numbers	DEMATEL, CFCS	In this paper, grey numbers were used to quantify expert judgments and create grey direct-relation matrices. A procedure was then performed to whitening the grey numbers using the CFCS method
Chang et al. [11]		√	√	GAME	AHP	The text shows the integration of the AHP method with grey relationship analysis. The GRA method was an element that allowed the selection of the most preferred decision option to be evaluated
Cui et al. [12]	√	√			DEMATEL, CFCS	In this paper, grey numbers were used to quantify expert judgements. Basic algebraic operations and a modified CFCS method were also used to determine their whitened values

(continued)

Table 3.6 (continued)

Article authors/ year	Position in the information analysis process			Methods used		Comments
	Preprocessor	Processor	Post-processor	GST	Other	
Dutta et al. [13]	√	√		Grey numbers	DEMATEL CFCS	The paper demonstrates a complex hybrid research methodology with the DEMATEL method using grey numbers as a central analytical element. In the preprocessing of the information, research strategies such as literature analysis and expert judgement were used, which were quantified using grey numbers. In post-processing, methods based on fuzzy logic were used
Ethirajan et al. [14]	√	√		Grey numbers	DEMATEL, CFCS	In the work, the central research method is the DEMATEL method using grey numbers. In preparation using grey numbers, expert assessments are quantified as a basis for further calculations. In post-processing, the method results from the DEMATEL method were used to develop a risk metric
Gangurde [15]		√		GAME	AHP	This paper shows the integration of the AHP method with grey relationship analysis. The GRA method in the final phase of the analytical process allowed the prioritisation of the different decision alternatives

(continued)

Table 3.6 (continued)

Article authors/ year	Position in the information analysis process			Methods used		Comments
	Preprocessor	Processor	Post-processor	GST	Other	
Ghosh and Bhattacharya [16]		√	√	GAME	MERC (Method based on the removal effects of criteria), CoCoSo (Combined compromi-sed solution)	The article discusses a hybrid decision-making methodology in the context of the problem of evaluating a selected group of companies. The methodology consisted of two stages. First, the criteria weights were determined using the method based on the removal effects of criteria (MERC), and then the combined compromised solution (CoCoSo) method was used to evaluate the individual companies against the adopted criteria. The CoCoSo method was integrated into the GRA
Gnanasekaran et al. [17]		√	√	GAME	AHP	The article shows the integration of GRA with the AHP method. The method was used to determine the criteria weights, while the grey relationship analysis was the basis for developing the ranking of decision alternatives

(continued)

Table 3.6 (continued)

Article authors/year	Position in the information analysis process			Methods used		Comments
	Preprocessor	Processor	Post-processor	GST	Other	
Govindan et al. [18]	√	√		Grey numbers	DEMATEL, CFCS	The grey DEMATEL method was used in the text. The input to the method was evaluated using grey numbers. This procedure allowed for the quantification of expert linguistic evaluations. Thus, it was reasonable to use basic grey algebraic operations and whitening procedures in the matrix computation process in DEMATEL
Jafari-Sadeghi et al. [19]		√		Grey numbers	Multi-objective mixed integer (MOMI)	This paper uses algebraic operations on grey numbers to develop a grey multi-objective mixed integer (GMOMI) model for use in project management issues
Hajiagha et al. [20]	√	√		Grey numbers	DEMATEL, CFCS	In this study, the grey DEMATEL method was used, where the grey numbers were used to quantify the linguistic assessments
Jaiswal et al. [21]	√	√		Grey numbers	DEMATEL, CFCS	The grey DEMATEL method was used using grey numbers and CFCS-based bleaching procedures

(continued)

Table 3.6 (continued)

Article authors/ year	Position in the information analysis process			Methods used		Comments
	Preprocessor	Processor	Post-processor	GST	Other	
Jamkhaneh et al. [22]	√	√		Grey numbers	DEMATEL, CFCS	The input data were expressed as grey numbers. Grey numbers were used in the matrix calculation procedures using the DEMATEL method. To simplify the calculations, the numbers were whitened using the CFCS method
Khan et al. [23]	√	√		Grey numbers	DEMATEL	The grey DEMATEL method was used. The input data were in the form of grey numbers. No whitening procedures were applied to simplify the matrix calculations
Kumar [24]	√	√		Grey fixed weight clustering method,	VIKOR, CFCS	This article integrates several grey methods and the VIKOR method to develop a classification model for factors that affect sustainable management in a selected group of companies. Grey numbers and CFCS whitening were used in data pre-processing. On the other hand, the core post-processing algorithm was developed using the VIKOR method and the grey fixed weight clustering method

(continued)

Table 3.6 (continued)

Article authors/ year	Position in the information analysis process			Methods used		Comments
	Preprocessor	Processor	Post-processor	GST	Other	
Luthra et al. [25]	√	√		Grey numbers	DEMATEL, CFCS	The input data were expressed as grey numbers. These numbers were used in the matrix calculation procedures in the DEMATEL method. To simplify the calculations, the numbers were whitened using the CFCS method
Mahdiraji et al. [26]	√	√		Grey numbers	DEMATEL, DANP (Decision Analytic Network Process), CoCoSo, CFCS	The research used a hybrid methodology integrating the grey DEMATEL method with the Decision Analytic Network Process (DANP) method. The grey DEMATEL method and DANP served as the core element of the analytical process. Grey numbers were used to quantify expert judgements in the preparation of the data. Then grey algebraic operations resulting from the DEMATEL method and CFCS whitening were performed on the data thus prepared. In post-processing the data, the CoCoSo method was used
Nguyen [27]	√			GM(1,1)	DEA	In this paper, grey predictive models are used to prepare data for the use of performance evaluation using the DEA method

(continued)

Table 3.6 (continued)

Article authors/ year	Position in the information analysis process			Methods used		Comments
	Preprocessor	Processor	Post-processor	GST	Other	
Nguyen [28]	√			GM(1,1)	Binary logistic model, EFA (Exploratory factor analysis)	In the text, a grey predictive model was used as a tool to forecast the states of selected characteristics that affect the supply chain. The grey model was complementary to classical statistical analyses and to analyses using SERVQUAL service quality assessment
Nguyen and Nguyen [29]	√			GM(1,1)	DEA	The results of the grey predictive model were used as input in the assessment of supplier performance using the DEA method
Nguyen and Tran [30]	√			GM(1,1)	DEA	The results of the grey predictive model were used as input to evaluate the efficiency of companies in terms of their ability to form strategic alliances. Efficiency was investigated using the DEA method
Ou [31]	√			GAME	DEMATEL	This article shows the integration of GRA with the DEMATEL method. Instead of the standard expert knowledge approach, the evaluation of the relationships between individual factors was determined using grey relational analysis

(continued)

Table 3.6 (continued)

Article authors/ year	Position in the information analysis process			Methods used		Comments
	Preprocessor	Processor	Post-processor	GST	Other	
Raj et al. [4]	√	√		Grey numbers	DEMATEL, CFCS	This paper shows another standard integration of grey numbers and the DEMATEL method. Grey numbers were used to quantify the expert data and then, after whitening with CFCS, for further matrix calculations
Sandeep et al. [32]		√	√	GAME	AHP	In this paper, the AHP method was used to determine the weights of the decision criteria, then the ranking of the individual decision options was obtained using the GRA method
Sangari et al. [33]	√	√		Grey numbers	ANP, DEMATEL, and CFCS	The paper shows the standard DEMATEL approach based on grey numbers. The DEMATEL results were used for further analyses using the ANP method
Singh et al. [34]	√	√		Grey numbers	DEMATEL, CFCS	The paper uses the most standard form of the grey DEMATEL method using grey numbers to quantify expert judgements
Singh et al. [35]	√	√		Grey numbers	DEMATEL, CFCS defuzzification method	As in other publications, the most standard form of the grey DEMATEL method was used, using grey numbers to quantify expert judgments

(continued)

Table 3.6 (continued)

Article authors/year	Position in the information analysis process			Methods used		Comments
	Preprocessor	Processor	Post-processor	GST	Other	
Tsai et al. [36]	√	√		GAME	AHP	A grey relational model was used to classify the decision options based on the weights determined by the AHP method
Wang et al. [37]		√		GAME	DEA	Grey relationship analysis was used to complement the DEA method. The data from both methods were then compared and subjected to further qualitative analysis
Wang et al. [38]		√		Grey numbers	AHP	In this paper, algebraic operations on grey numbers were implemented directly and without whitening. This implementation involved the quantification of expert judgements and matrix calculations in the AHP method
Wu et al. [39]	√	√		GAME	AHP	A grey relational model was used to classify the decision options based on the weights determined by the AHP method
Xu et al. [40]	√			Grey numbers	Rough Set Theory (RST)	Grey numbers were used to develop inputs to the rough set theory (RST) information model

(continued)

Table 3.6 (continued)

Article authors/year	Position in the information analysis process			Methods used		Comments
	Preprocessor	Processor	Post-processor	GST	Other	
Yang et al. [41]	√			GAME	Interpretative Structural Model (ISM)	The GRA model was used to develop input to the matrix of influencing factors
Yuan and Chen [42]			√	GAME	Simple Additive Weights (SAW), Fuzzy Set Theory, AHP	In this paper, the GRA model is used to classify decision options and compare them with the rankings obtained using the Simple Additive Weights (SAW) method
Zhu et al. [43]	√	√		Grey numbers	DEMATEL, CFCS	As in other publications, the most standard form of the grey DEMATEL method was used, using grey numbers to quantify expert judgments
Zolfani et al. [44]		√	√	Grey numbers	FAHP, TOPSIS	In this paper, the weights were determined using AHP procedures and fuzzy logic elements. The data were then used in the TOPSIS method using grey-algebraic operations in computational processes

- Very little use is made of data-driven decision rule discovery using rough set theory (RST) and GST methods, which may be due to the fact that the process of quantifying data using grey numbers does not generally increase the efficiency, effectiveness, and ease of creating and analysing information systems in RST.
- Statistical methods were combined to a small extent with grey analytical methods and, in principle, statistical analysis and analysis using GST methods could be carried out separately as there was no data flow between them; the nature of these analyses was essentially comparative and triangulatory.

In management research, the main use of GST is a hybrid approach. It mainly consists of combining grey methods with other analytical solutions. Also important is the consequent fact that GST methods are not a stand-alone tool for analysing research problems. The problem here is the metaphorical nature of the notion of grey as prevalent in the literature and the methodologically poorly developed issue of analysing small data sets. In particular, the issue here is that representative research results are derived from an empirical base. GST methods can use a small number of data as a result of their formal properties, however, additional methodological procedures related to the triangulation procedure are needed to authenticate the results. Hence, with these shortcomings in mind, GST methods are complemented by more established and mature research methodologies. Furthermore, this methodological aspect results in the main application area of GST being expert-based research strategies using hybrid research methods.

References

1. Chiu, W.-Y., Tzeng, G.-H., Li, H.-L.: Improving the E-store business model for satisfying customers' needs using a hybrid MCDM combined DANP with grey relational model. In: Phillips-Wren, G., Jain, L.C., Nakamatsu, K., Howlett, R.J. (eds.) Advances in Intelligent Decision Technologies, pp. 113–121. Springer Berlin, Heidelberg (2010)
2. Huang, C.-Y., Shyu, J.Z., Tzeng, G.-H.: Reconfiguring the innovation policy portfolios for Taiwan's SIP Mall industry. Technovation **27**(12), 744–765 (2007)
3. Nguyen, N.-T.: Optimizing factors for accuracy of forecasting models in food processing industry: a context of cacao manufacturers in Vietnam. Indust. Eng. Manag. Syst. **18**(4), 808–824 (2019)
4. Raj, A., Mukherjee, A.A., de Sousa Jabbour, A.B.L., Srivastava, S.K.: Supply chain management during and post-COVID-19 pandemic: mitigation strategies and practical lessons learned. J. Bus. Res. **142**, 1125–1139 (2022)
5. Yang, T., Wen, Y.-F., Wang, F.-F.: Evaluation of robustness of supply chain information-sharing strategies using a hybrid Taguchi and multiple criteria decision-making method. Int. J. Prod. Econ. **134**(2), 458–466 (2011)
6. Pan, M.-C., Lee, T.-R., Anbuudayasankar, S.P., Ganesh, K.: Key success factors of holding exhibitions for the exhibition organisers using dramaturgy model and grey relational analysis. Int. J. Tour. Policy **5**(4), 269–295 (2014)
7. Ansari, Z.N., Kant, R., Shankar, R.: Remanufacturing supply chain: an analysis of performance indicator areas. Int. J. Prod. Perform. Manag. **71**(1), 25–57 (2022)
8. Bai, C., Sarkis, J.: A grey-based DEMATEL model for evaluating business process management critical success factors. Int. J. Prod. Econ. **146**(1), 281–292 (2013)

9. Bai, C., Sarkis, J., Wei, X., Koh, L.: Evaluating ecological sustainable performance measures for supply chain management. Supply Chain Manag. **17**(1), 78–92 (2012)
10. Banerjee, T., et al.: Analyzing organizational barriers towards building post-pandemic supply chain resilience in Indian MSMEs: a grey-DEMATEL approach. Benchmark. Int. J. (2022)
11. Chang, C.-W., Wu, C.-R., Lin, J.-Y.: Multi-approach model for selection of SCMS in semiconductor industry upstream. J. Grey Syst. **20**(2), 135–148 (2008)
12. Cui, L., et al.: Exploring critical factors of green business failure based on grey-decision making trial and evaluation laboratory (DEMATEL). J. Bus. Res. **98**, 450–461 (2019)
13. Dutta, P., Talaulikar, S., Xavier, V., Kapoor, S.: Fostering reverse logistics in India by prominent barrier identification and strategy implementation to promote circular economy. J. Clean. Prod. **294** (2021)
14. Ethirajan, M., et al.: Analysing the risks of adopting circular economy initiatives in manufacturing supply chains. Bus Strat Environ **30**(1), 204–236 (2021)
15. Gangurde, S.R.: Benchmarking the best factory data collection system (FDC) using AHP-GRA method. Benchmarking **23**(2), 359–370 (2016)
16. Ghosh, S., Bhattacharya, M.: Analyzing the impact of COVID-19 on the financial performance of the hospitality and tourism industries: an ensemble MCDM approach in the Indian context. Int. J. Contemp. Hospit. Manag. **34**(8), 3113–3142 (2022)
17. Gnanasekaran, S., Velappan, S., Ayappan, S.: An integrated model for supplier selection: an automobile industry case study. Int. J. Serv. Operat. Manag. **6**(1), 89–105 (2010)
18. Govindan, K., et al.: Structural model for analysis of key performance indicators for sustainable manufacturer-supplier collaboration: a grey-decision-making trial and evaluation laboratory-based approach. Bus. Strat. Environ. **30**(4), 1702–1722 (2021)
19. Jafari-Sadeghi, V., Mahdiraji, H.A., Busso, D., Yahiaoui, D.: Towards agility in international high-tech SMEs: Exploring key drivers and main outcomes of dynamic capabilities. Technol. Forecast. Soc. Change 174 (2022)
20. Hajiagha, S.H.R., Akrami, H., Hashemi, S.S., Mahdiraji, H.A.: An integer grey goal programming for project time, cost and quality trade-off. Eng. Econ. **26**(1), 93–100 (2015)
21. Jaiswal, P., Singh, A., Misra, S.C., Kumar, A.: Barriers in implementing lean manufacturing in Indian SMEs: a multi-criteria decision-making approach. J. Model. Manag. **16**(1), 339–356 (2021)
22. Jamkhaneh, H.B., Shahin, A., Parkouhi SV, Shahin R (2022) The new concept of quality in the digital era: a human resource empowerment perspective. TQM J. **34**(1), 125–144 (2022)
23. Khan, S., Haleem, A., Khan, M.I.: Enablers to implement circular initiatives in the supply chain: a grey DEMATEL method. Glob. Bus. Rev. (2020)
24. Kumar, A.: Transition management theory-based policy framework for analysing environmentally responsible freight transport practices. J. Clean. Prod. 294 (2021)
25. Luthra, S., et al.: Industry 4.0 as an enabler of sustainability diffusion in supply chain: an analysis of influential strength of drivers in an emerging economy. Int. J. Prod. Res. **58**(5), 1505–1521 (2020)
26. Mahdiraji, H.A., Beheshti, M., Jafari-Sadeghi, V., Garcia-Perez, A.: What drives inter-organisational knowledge management? The cause and effect analysis using a multi-layer multi-criteria decision-making framework. J. Knowl. Manag. **26**(9), 2195–2221 (2022)
27. Nguyen, N.-T.: Performance evaluation in strategic alliances: a case of Vietnamese construction industry. Glob. J. Flex. Syst. Manag. **21**(1), 85–99 (2020)
28. Nguyen, H.-K.: A 3-dimensional frame of reference for prevention of risk in supply chain. J. Risk Financ. Manag. **15**(3) (2022)
29. Nguyen, P., Nguyen, N.T.: Using optimization algorithms of DEA and grey system theory in strategic partner selection: an empirical study in Vietnam steel industry. Cogent. Bus. Manag. **7**(1) (2020)
30. Nguyen, N.-T., Tran, T.-T.: A study of the strategic alliance for Vietnam domestic pharmaceutical industry: a dynamic integration of a hybrid DEA and GM (1,1) approach. J. Grey Syst. **30**(4), 134–151 (2018)

31. Ou, Y.-C.: Using a hybrid decision-making model to evaluate the sustainable development performance of high-tech listed companies. J. Bus. Econ. Manag. **17**(3), 331–346 (2016)
32. Sandeep, M., Kumanan, S., Vinodh, S.: Supplier selection using combined AHP and GRA for a pump manufacturing industry. Int. J. Logist. Syst. Manag. **10**(1), 40–52 (2011)
33. Sangari, M.S., Nikkhoo, F., Khoshsirat, M.: An integrated GRA-DEMATEL-ANP framework for evaluation of barriers to implementation of green supply chain management in manufacturing industries. Int. J. Bus. Syst. Res. **14**(2), 228–248 (2020)
34. Singh, R.K., Luthra, S., Mangla, S.K., Uniyal, S.: Applications of information and communication technology for sustainable growth of SMEs in India food industry. Resour. Conserv. Recycl. **147**, 10–18 (2019)
35. Singh, A., Thakkar, J., Jenamani, M.: An integrated Grey-DEMATEL approach for evaluating ICT adoption barriers in manufacturing SMEs analysing Indian MSMEs. J. Enterprise Inform. Manag.
36. Tsai, H.-Y., Huang, B.-H., Wang, A.-S.: Combining AHP and GRA model for evaluation property-liability insurance companies to rank. J. Grey Syst. **20**(1), 65–78 (2008)
37. Wang, S., Noe, R.A., Wang, Z.-M.: Motivating knowledge sharing in knowledge management systems. J. Manag. **40**, 978–1009 (2011)
38. Wang, X., Chen, W., Shang, J., Yang, S.: Foreign markets expansion for air medical transport business. J. Operat. Res. Soc. **69**(7), 1146–1159 (2018)
39. Wu, C.-R., Lin, C.-T., Tsai, P.-H.: Evaluating business performance of wealth management banks. European J. Operat. Res. **207**(2), 971–979 (2010)
40. Xu, Z., Liu, X., Bai, C., Hu, L.: Green marketing: a grey-based rough set theory analysis of activities. Int. J. Innov. Sci. **7**(1), 27–37 (2015)
41. Yang, Z., Guo, X., Sun, J., Zhang, Y.: Contextual and organizational factors in sustainable supply chain decision making: grey relational analysis and interpretative structural modelling. Environ. Dev. Sustain. **23**(8), 12056–12076 (2021)
42. Yuan, B.J.C., Chen, J.K.C.: Adopting information systems for China enterprise investing using the grey relation analysis. Int. J. Value Chain Manag. **1**(4), 416–438 (2007)
43. Zhu, Q., Sarkis, J., Geng, Y.: Barriers to environmentally-friendly clothing production among Chinese apparel companies. Asian Bus. Manag. **10**(3), 425–452 (2011)
44. Zolfani, S.H., Rezaeiniya, N., Edmundas, P., Zavadskas, E.K.: Decision making on advertising strategy selection based on life cycle of products by applying FAHP and TOPSIS GREY: growth stage perspective; a case about food industry in Iran. Eng. Econ. **23**(5), 471–484 (2012)
45. Zolfani, S.H., Rezaeiniya, N., Pourhossein, M., Zavadskas, K.: Decision making on advertisement strategy selection based on life cycle of products by applying FAHP and TOPSIS GREY: growth stage perspective; a case about food industry in IRAN. Eng. Econ. **23** (2013)

Chapter 4
Model for the Selection of Grey Research Methods in Management Sciences

4.1 Basic Assumptions and General Scheme of the Grey Methods Selection Model in Management Science Research

The starting point in the proper selection of grey methods in the context of a given research problem is to consider the validity of their application. To this end, it is necessary to examine whether the formal properties of the data held or potentially obtainable data can be expressed using the mathematical apparatus of grey systems theory. Identification of the validity of GST application should be made based on the guidelines provided by the procedure shown in Fig. 4.1.

The first step in the procedure to justify the choice of GST methods in research processes must be the operationalisation of the research problem. It consists of identifying the characteristics of the phenomenon or object under study in terms of the main research objective and the research questions posed. Identified features and their states allow the development of an abstract information model. On the basis of this information model, analytical operations are then carried out to explain or explore the investigated fragment of reality. As a result of the operationalisation of the study, we should answer several questions on the basis of the constructed model. Firstly: Is the amount of data available to collect relatively small in the context of the requirements of statistical methods? Second: are the data imprecise and incomplete? These questions essentially boil down to the problem of the quality of the survey sample taken in terms of unambiguity and representativeness of the data. Unambiguity is the result of the use of strong measurement scales when measuring the characteristics analysed, while representativeness is the result of the procedure for selecting units for the research sample. If the data collected are of the required quality, it makes sense to use a statistical approach. It would then be a methodological

The original version of the chapter has been revised. A correction to this chapter can be found at https://doi.org/10.1007/978-981-97-2413-0_5

R. Mierzwiak, *Methodological Aspects of Grey Systems Theory in Management Research*, Series on Grey System, https://doi.org/10.1007/978-981-97-2413-0_4

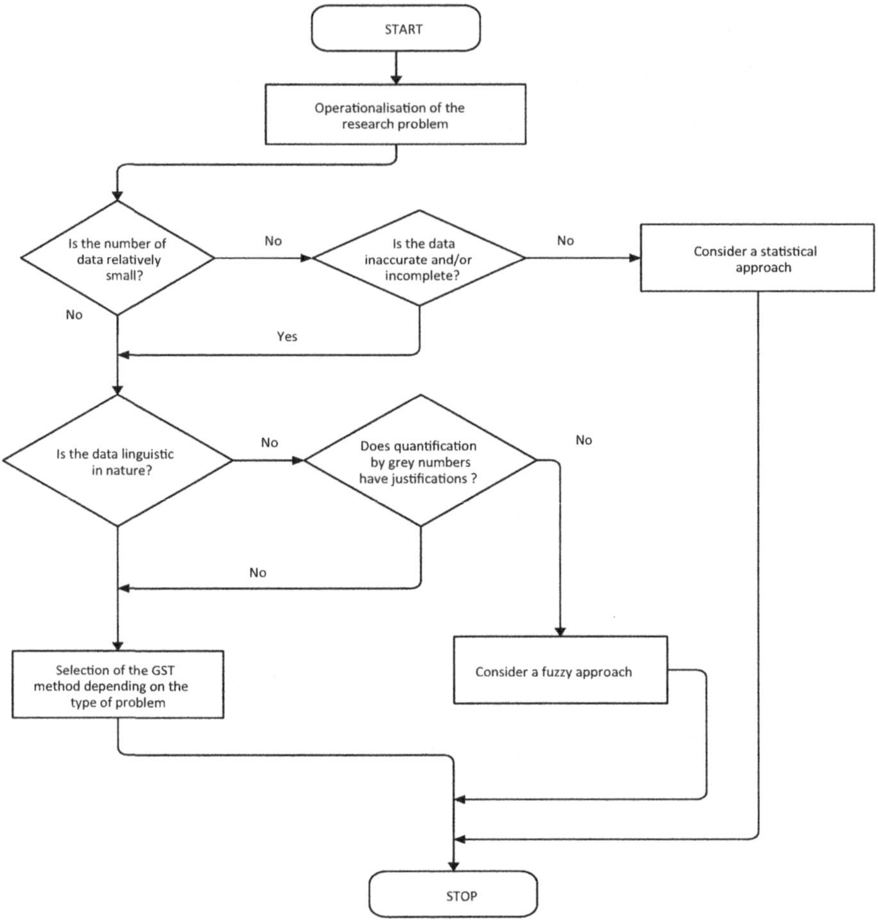

Fig. 4.1 Procedure to justify the selection of the grey analytical approach in the study

error to analyse the data using GST methods. This is justified in that many GST techniques at the level of formal structure have assumptions that, when analysing larger numbers of data, can cause logical and computational paradoxes. However, if the data do not meet the assumptions for the requirements when using statistical methods, then GST can be considered as an alternative approach. However, another important issue arises here that needs to be resolved: the nature of the data collected. If they are predominantly linguistic and expressed using natural language, then the question must be asked about their ability to be quantified using grey or fuzzy numbers. If the data can be expressed using fuzzy numbers and the form of the membership function is determinable or substantively justifiable, then a fuzzy approach should be used, thus dispensing with GST methods. Otherwise, when we do not have a rationale for inferring the form of the membership function through a quantification process, one must adopt a quantification approach using a transformation function F:

$\{S(L), R\} \rightarrow \{\otimes S, \leq\}$ based on a selected continuum of grey numbers. Regarding fuzzy logic and membership functions, a detailed issue is the problem of similarity to whitening functions [1]. This problem, however, needs to be analysed in the next step: in the selection of GST methods, taking into account the detailed context of the problem at hand. It should be signalled that this is important, especially in the modelling of processes of a decision-making nature.

Taking into account the procedure presented and assuming the division of management research into exploratory and exploratory, we can conclude that the domain of grey methods will be mainly exploratory research (Exploratory Data Analysis). They should be characterised by the following [2], pp. 20–23:

- They are mainly aimed at a preliminary analysis of the relevant features, relationships, and mechanisms of a phenomenon, while they will be minimally conclusive on the basis of a verification or falsification approach.
- They have a flexible and variable scope of research and a simple and little formalised data collection procedure.
- They operate on small, purposeful, and subjective research samples.
- The quantitative analysis in these studies should be complemented by qualitative research, taking into account the methodological assumptions of triangulation, thus increasing the reliability of the results obtained.

However, when grey methods are used in exploratory research, although they are feasible, the assumption regarding the representativeness of the research sample must be met. However, the use of other methods, such as nonparametric statistical methods, is recommended.

The spectrum of methods in GST is broad and strongly differentiated. At the most general level of their classification, we can distinguish between the methods inherent to GST and the integrated methods. The former are methods inherent only in GST, while integrated methods are hybrid methods that combine other analytical approaches with classical grey methods and theoretical constructs. Among the classical inherent methods we can include Grey Inciedence Analysis (GIA) models, predictive models (GM), and decision models. Hybrid models mainly include network models and models that, by means of grey numbers or, to a lesser extent, other GST methods, modify original concepts derived from other strands of uncertain information analysis. Like inherent methods, hybrid methods need to be systematised in terms of their usefulness and possible scope of application in management science research. This should take into account their structure and the detailed specificity of their methodological assumptions.

4.2 Guidelines for Grey Incidence Analysis Models

Grey incident analysis (GIA) is a group of methods in grey systems theory that investigate relationships between variables. In mathematical terms, GIA methods are nothing more than the study of geometric similarity between series of data.

Thus, as can be seen, the relationships between data are equated with their geometric similarity. A proper understanding of this issue is fundamental to understanding the capabilities and limitations of GIA. Taking this into account and the methodological recommendations made in the earlier discussion of GIA (see Sect. 2.2), the research process using GIA can be reduced to the guidelines provided by the procedure shown in Fig. 4.2.

The research process, regardless of whether GIA models are used, should begin with the conceptualisation of the study. This stage is to clearly define the research problems, the scope of the study, the research hypotheses, and the desired objectives

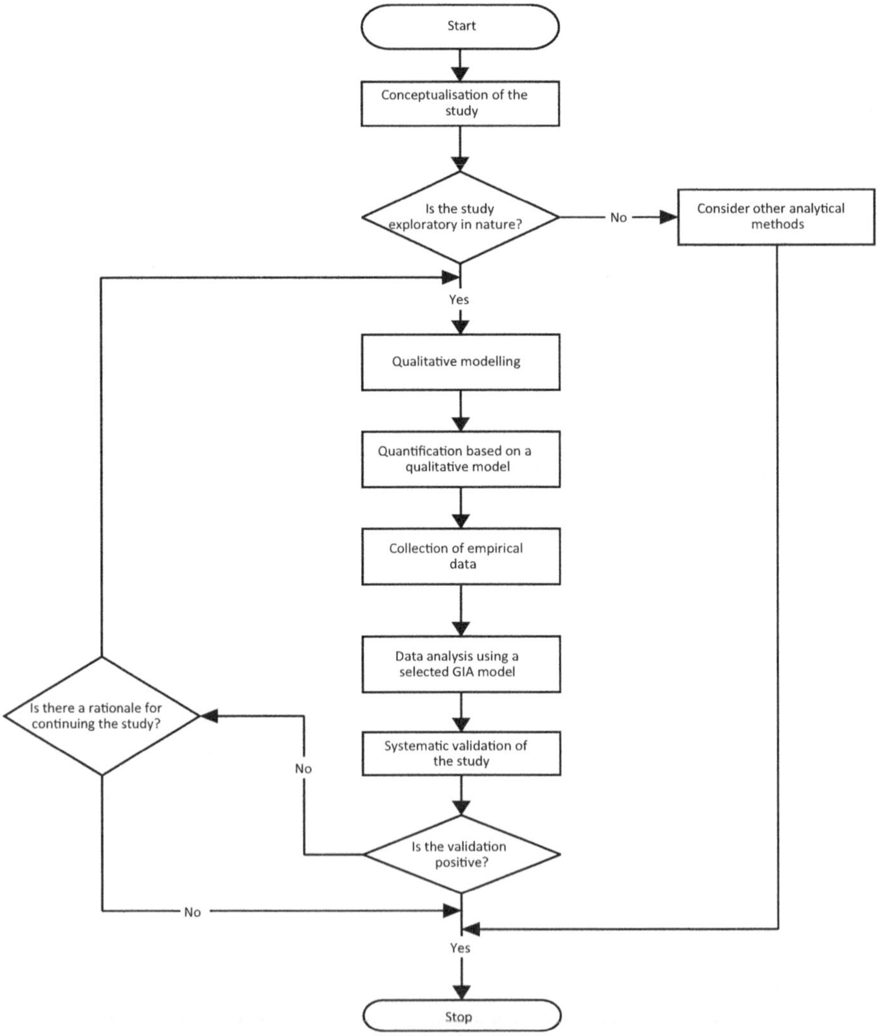

Fig. 4.2 Procedure for proceeding with the GIA testing process

of the study. In this stage, the study transforms from an intuitive and unstructured phase into a systematic and structured process. If a specific research problem is framed in a systemic form and the main goal of the research is to analyse the relationships between features in this system, we can consider GIA models in the process. These models in particular can be used when the study being designed is exploratory in nature. This is because, in this type of research, the research samples are purposive in nature, and the results obtained are intended to provide preliminary insights into the problematic area. In many cases where the research results are intended to support rapid managerial decisions, this type of research is dominant. In this type of research, we have empirical material of limited quality in terms of its representativeness or other properties required in statistical models. GIA models will therefore be limited in their applications to studies of an exploratory nature, whereas when the design is to be exploratory, statistical inference methods are clearly preferable.

Once the study has been conceptualised, the next step will be a qualitative analysis of the research problem in question. The result of this analysis must be a description of the problem in terms of an input–output model. The qualitative specification of the input–output at this stage does not need to contain complete information on the possible states of the individual features. It is limited only to the identification of features by means of relatively unambiguous linguistic formulas. At this stage, it is also important to identify the temporal characteristics of the system in question. This involves answering the following questions:

- whether the characteristics under study will be analysed in terms of the variability of their states over time?
- whether the characteristics under study will be analysed across a set of objects or criteria at a given point in time?

An affirmative answer to the first question classifies the model in question as a dynamic model and the second as a static model. An example of a study in which a dynamic model can be used is a study of the relationship between the level of employee engagement and job satisfaction in a given company over the last 10 years. A static study, on the other hand, is, for example, an examination of the relationship between employee engagement and job satisfaction in a given year in a sample of 10 companies or the relationship between data from these companies in terms of a set of selected criteria affecting employee engagement and job satisfaction at a given point in time.

Having a set of input and output features, the next step is to quantify them. It requires a more detailed understanding of the features by identifying for each feature the range of possible states of it and then assigning a quantitative feature to it. Operationally, this can be done by measuring, scaling, or constructing indicators. The quantification process is the basis for the next step, which is the collection of empirical data according to the assumptions arising from the exploratory nature of the research carried out and the principles of the adopted quantification formula. This step should formally lead to the collection of empirical material in the form of a data sequence. The data sequence can be organised in different ways depending on whether we are dealing with dynamic or static modelling and whether the data in the sequence concern a single object or a set of objects. Taking this into account, we can distinguish the following types of sequences used in GIA: time sequence, criterion sequence, and horizontal sequence. These sequences are precisely defined in Definitions 4.1 and 4.2.

Definition 4.1 Suppose $X_i = (x_i(1), x_i(2), \ldots, x_i(n))$ is the set of numbers describing some object O, then:

1. If k is a moment in time and $x_i(k)$ is the numerically expressed state of the feature x_i of the object O at the moment k, then a data set like $X_i = (x_i(1), x_i(2), \ldots, x_i(n))$ is called a time sequence.
2. If k is the ordinal number of the criterion according to which the object O is analysed and $x_i(k)$ is the numerically expressed state of the feature x_i relative to k -then we call such a data set as $X_i = (x_i(1), x_i(2), \ldots, x_i(n))$ a criterion sequence.

Note: $k = 1, 2, \ldots, n; i \in N; n \in N.$

Definition 4.2 Suppose that $X_i = (x_i(1), x_i(2), \ldots, x_i(n))$ is a set of numbers describing some set of objects $O = (o_1, o_2, \ldots, o_m)$ in such a way that $x_i(k)$ is the numerically expressed state of the feature x_i for k this object, then $X_i = (x_i(1), x_i(2), \ldots, x_i(n))$ is called horizontal sequence.

The collection of empirical data in the form of data sequences, as formally described above, makes it possible to select an appropriate GIA model. Table 4.2 can be used for this selection. Characterises the most popular models in the literature according to the following criteria: the type of model in terms of its temporal structure, the formal properties of the model resulting from its mathematical structure, the feature that operationalises the study of relationships between variables and the type of operator used between variables.

The first criterion, the type of model in terms of its temporal structure, takes two possibilities. These are dynamic models, in which sequences are temporal, and static models, in which data sequences are horizontal or criterion sequences. A GIA model can have these two possibilities simultaneously. Indeed, this is not an exclusionary division.

Criterion two, on the other hand, has four possibilities, and they are not mutually exclusive. The point is that the model under analysis can simultaneously exhibit all the possibilities, i.e.: wholeness, normality, pair symmetry, and closeness. In intuitive terms, wholeness can be interpreted as the property by which the outcome of the relationship between two specific variables in some system is also influenced by all other variables considered in the study. Normality, on the other hand, can be intuitively interpreted as the property by which the results of an analysis are synthesised on a scale from 0 to 1. The closer the value is to 1, the stronger the relationship between the variables. Symmetry, on the other hand, is a property whereby if we have two variables X_i and $X_{j,}$ then for the relationship $X_i \rightarrow X_j$ and $X_j \rightarrow X_i$ the value of the relationship indicator in the GIA model is the same. On the other hand, for the property closeness we can interpret it as the closeness between some variables X_i and X_j, with this closeness being determined not from the original data, but from the data obtained by preprocessing with the grey operator. If the GIA model takes this aspect into account and behaves in such a way that in the geometric interpretation of the data on the plane: the smaller the distance between the points representing the data, the higher the relationship index in the model, then in that case we can say that the model retains the closeness property. We formally detail all the properties of GIA models discussed in Sect. 2.2.

The third criterion characterising a given GIA model is the feature that operationalises the concept of the relationship between the variables under study. The first possibility in this criterion is the geometric similarity between the shape of the lines formed in two-dimensional space based on the points representing the data sequence. The second possibility is to operationalise by means of the dynamics of value changes at individual points in the data sequence with respect to a common anchor baseline value. A third possibility is an approach to operationalisation based on the Euclidean distance between corresponding points in the temporal sequence. The possibilities in this criterion are only partially mutually exclusive. It is acceptable for a given model to consider geometric shape and rate of change simultaneously, while it is not possible for a distance-based model to use an approach based on similarity of shape and rate of change.

The fourth criterion by which GIA models have been characterised is the type of operator used in the model. For this criterion, we have five possibilities: inintialing operator (D_1), averaging operator (D_2), interval operator (D_3), reversing operator (D_4), reciprocating operator (D_5). The collection of these operators allows the data to be transformed according to the theoretical assumptions derived from the grey space axioms of the distributive understanding of grey. These operators can be used independently or in combination in applications. On the basis of the theoretical and formal properties of the operators, as well as experiences from the practice of their application in management research problems, a matrix for the selection of grey inciedence operators can be constructed. It is shown in Table 4.1.

The correct choice and combination of operators allow the desired properties of each GIA model to be obtained. Table 4.1, together with the mathematical properties of the operators shown in Subsection 2.2, is an integral complement to the described

Table 4.1 Selection matrix for grey operators in GIA models

D_j	D_i				
	D_1	D_2	D_3	D_4	D_5
D_1	×	×	×	×	√
D_2	×	×	×	×	√
D_3	×	×	×	√	√
D_4	√	√	√	×	×
D_5	√	√	√	×	×

Table 4.2 Characteristics of the basic GIA models

Model GIA	Criteria													
	Type of model in the context of time		Formal properties of the model resulting from its mathematical structure				A feature that operationalises the study of relationships between variables			Used type of grey operators[a]				
	Dynamic	Static	Wholeness	Normality	Symmetry	Closeness	Geometric shape	Pace of change	Distance between points	D_1	D_2	D_3	D_4	D_5
Deng's model of grey incidence analysis [3, 4] and derived models: weighted degree of grey incidence [5], entropy degree of grey incidence [6]	√	√	√	√	× (Only pair symmetry)	√	×	×	√	√	√	√	√	√
Absolute of grey incidence [7] and the derived model of grey similar incidence degree [3]	√ (This model uses a specific operator that subtracts the value of the first item from each value in the data sequence)	× (To a limited extent, when the order of objects or criteria in a horizontal or criterion sequence is of merit)	×	√	√	√	√	×	×	×	×	×	×	×
Relative degree of grey incidence [7] and derived model of grey closeness degree of incidence [8]	√	× (To a limited extent, when the order of objects or criteria in a horizontal or criterion sequence is of merit)	×	√	√	√	×	√	×	√	×	×	×	×

(continued)

Table 4.2 (continued)

Model GIA	Criteria													
	Type of model in the context of time		Formal properties of the model resulting from its mathematical structure				A feature that operationalises the study of relationships between variables			Used type of grey operators[a]				
	Dynamic	Static	Wholeness	Normality	Symmetry	Closeness	Geometric shape	Pace of change	Distance between points	D_1	D_2	D_3	D_4	D_5
Synthetic degree of grey incidence [7]	√ (Due to the hybridity of the model, resulting from combining the absolute and relative degrees of grey incidence models. the operator typical of the latter model is used and the operator D_1)	× (To a limited extent, when the order of objects or criteria in a horizontal or criterion sequence is of merit)	×	√	√	√	√ (The impact of this criterion is governed by a normalised impact factor, as the model is a hybrid of relative and absolute grey incidence)	√ (The impact of this criterion is governed by a normalised impact factor, as the model is a hybrid of relative and absolute grey incidence)	×	√	×	×	×	×
Panel models, e.g.: grey relational degree model for panel data [9]. These are models where the data are represented as a time series, where the elements of the series are matrices of data describing sets of objects in a cross-section of the criteria data set	√	×	×	√	√	√	√ (Measured by a model-specific measure reflecting the geometric similarity of the planes)	√ (Measured by a model-specific measure reflecting the dynamics of change of a plane relative to a chosen reference point in space)	√ Measured by a model-specific measure reflecting the distance between two planes	×	×	×	×	×
										Not applicable				

[a] (D_1), averaging operator (D_2), interval operator (D_3), reversing operator (D_4), reciprocating operator (D_5)

possible states of the discussed fourth criterion characterising GIA models. It is therefore complementary to Table 4.2 that characterises the GIA models in general.

Once a suitable GIA model has been selected for a given research problem structure and calculations have been carried out to obtain results that correspond to the research questions and hypotheses, the next step is to systematically validate the research process by confronting new empirical material or research results on the same empirical material but analysed using other methods. Validation thus boils down to the use of a triangulation approach. Triangulation in the context of GIA methods should first concern the research data. In this case, the research should be conducted again using the GIA model, but for a new research sample. The selection of a new research sample can take into account two cases. The first is a different temporal moment of data collection, but the same range of study objects. The second case, on the other hand, is the same temporal moment of the data collected, but a different group of objects under study. An example for the first case, i.e. a different temporal moment—the same range of objects—could be the study of some dependency occurring on a given group of enterprises in successive years. On the other hand, the second case, i.e. the same moment in time—different group of objects, can be illustrated by the example of research carried out in a given year on several different groups of enterprises included in the general population defined in the study. These two cases mark two different orientations of the research process. The first case directs the research process towards the identification and description of relationships at a given point in time. The second, on the other hand, is an approach that emphasises and takes into account the dynamics of change that occur in the research object over time. These two approaches understand the concept of systematicity in a different way in the context of validation. The first sees systematicity as an ordered process of learning about the general population. The second, on the other hand, understands systematicity as: an iterative process of measuring and providing new data over time that gives credence to the research results obtained.

The question of research sampling raised relates to the context of data triangulation. However, there are other forms of it, namely research method triangulation and researcher triangulation. Triangulation of research methods in research using GIA is nothing more than the examination of relationships between variables by other methods. Here it naturally comes to mind that the use of statistical methods is expedient. However, one has to be very careful, because we use the grey approach precisely because the conditions for the use of statistical methods do not exist. Hence, it is very easy for the researcher to fall into a logical contradiction. Another important problem is that even if we use a different methodological approach, the results will hardly be comparable to those obtained using GIA methods. Their formal commonality may be impossible or will have to be based on subjective expert judgments or subjective conclusions drawn directly by the researcher. As for researcher triangulation, this is more likely to be used and relevant in the context of the qualitative modelling of the study and to a lesser extent during the conceptualisation of the study and its quantification. These are areas where researcher subjectivity can distort the results of the study. It is therefore worthwhile, in the case of research where difficulties are suspected in these areas due to the complexity of the phenomenon, measurement difficulties, or precision in the qualitative and quantitative description in the study, to apply the procedure of researcher triangulation. It will eliminate the uncertainties of the study arising from the creative, heuristic, and subjective initial phases of the research process. It is worth noting that the procedure for using GIA methods is iterative. That is, the negative validation results force a rethinking of the entire study design. This iterative nature can, on the one hand, validate the results obtained and, on the other, guide the creation of new areas of research exploration.

In summary, research using GIA should be exploratory in nature. In the literature, in a nonexplicit way, GIA methods in management research have such a character. Their results can be used to design exploratory research in observational or experimental terms. Such a sequence of exploratory and exploratory research, due to the complex subject matter of research in the management sciences, is very common in the context of purely scientific research. In managerial activities, however, exploratory research alone can be a sufficient basis for management decisions, as this research represents a compromise between cost, time, and quality of the results obtained for decision-makers. Hence, GIA methods, in addition to their applications in research for purely cognitive use, can be of great importance in research of an implementation nature in management practice.

4.3 Guidelines for the Application of Grey Predictive Models

Forecasting and its methodological status may provoke a discussion important for identifying limitations in the study of the behaviour of complex economic, social, or managerial systems. However, this does not change the fact that, given research and economic practice, forecasting methods are widely used. Therefore, taking into account the methodological remarks formulated earlier with regard to grey forecasting models shown in Sect. 2.3 and the specificity of forecasting in the management sciences, we can reduce the process of using grey forecasting models to the iterative analytical procedure shown in Fig. 4.3.

The first stage is linguistic modelling, which involves developing a conceptualisation in a given natural language of the system under study, the states of which the researcher wishes to forecast. The result of this stage should be a qualitative description understood as a set of identified relevant features of the given system. These features, due to the heuristic nature of this stage, should be formulated as linguistic features, i.e. those whose state is identified as a natural language utterance. Thus, the verbal description of a system is not an arbitrary linguistic description, but should be an information model of the system in the form of a set of features that retrospectively, objectively, and factually represent the current state of the system under study. It should also be mentioned that the scope of the description should characterise the system as a whole and its components.

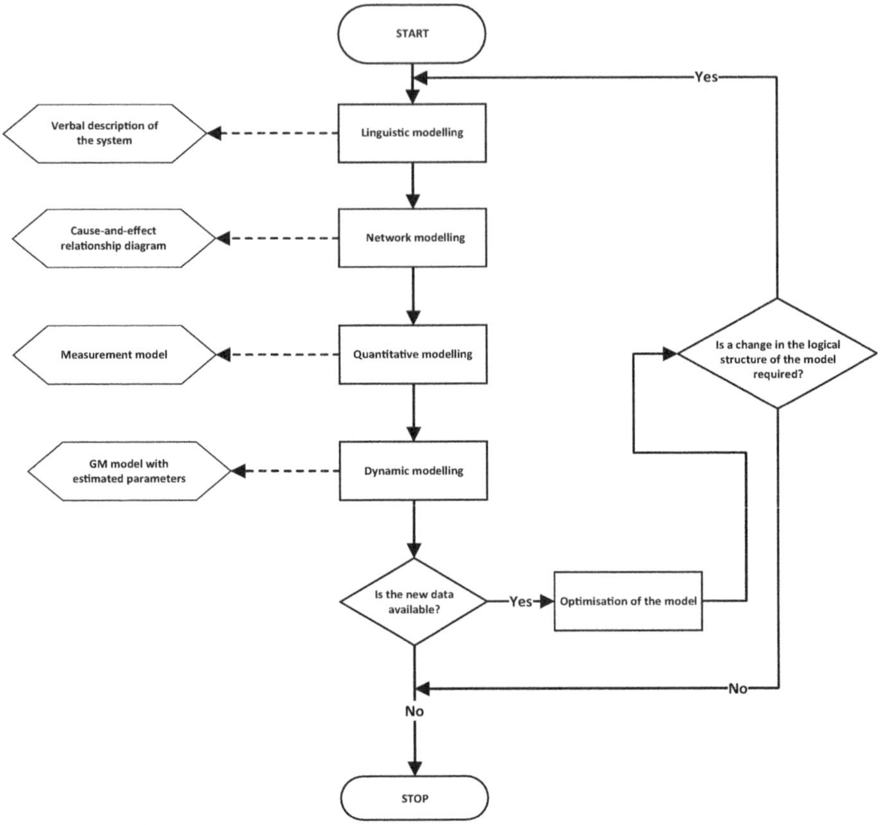

Fig. 4.3 Procedure for proceeding with the research process using predictive models

The second stage is network modelling, the essence of which is the transformation of the linguistic model into a network model. This process aims to find causal relationships between quality characteristics across the system. The aim is to transform the multiplicative nature of the linguistic model into a system model that takes into account the relationships and mechanisms of the analysed system. The result of this stage is the development of an open system diagram with identified inputs and outputs and the structure of the system in the context of cause-and-effect relationships that occur between the characteristics of individual subsystems.

The next stage is quantitative modelling, the aim of which is to develop a model for quantifying the linguistic features that characterise the inputs and outputs in the system under analysis. This stage can be reduced to the development of a measurement model that allows changes in the system to be expressed in terms of time sequences representing the input and output of the system.

Having a quantitative model at hand in the next step, the aim is to select an appropriate grey predictive model. From the point of view of research problems in management science, the default option should be a GM model (1, 1). This is because forecasting problems in these sciences, as in all social sciences, can be justified in terms of general direction and identification of more qualitative than quantitative patterns. Hence, precise determination of future states of social systems in coordinate time and with high accuracy is difficult or even impossible. Thus, using the basic simplest model and treating it as a basis for qualitatively identifying trends in the phenomenon or system under analysis makes pragmatic sense and can economise the research process. Of course, it is possible to use other models which, in selected aspects of detail, may be better suited to a given forecasting problem than a model of $GM(1, 1)$. Model $GM(1, 1)$ and the most popular forecasting models in the literature are shown in Table 4.3. It is based on the classification concept developed and elaborated by Xie [10, 11].

Once a predictive model has been selected, the next step is to collect empirical data to estimate its parameters, together with determining the estimation errors. These errors can be estimated by comparing the results simulated by the model with the empirical values based on which the model was constructed. Taking the standard

Table 4.3 Characteristics of basic grey prediction models

Type	Model name	Areas of application of the model	Source/author
Group models $GM(1, 1)$	Even Grey Model (EGM)	Default model in management science applications. In the literature, when talking about a model $GM(1, 1)$, is assumed by default to refer to the EGM. The model is applicable to: non-exponental sequence, fluctuating sequence	Deng [3, 4, 12]
	Original Difference Grey Model (ODGM)	This model is mainly applicable when we are dealing with a sequence of temporal data meeting the assumptions of a homogeneous exponential sequence	Liu et al. [13, 14]
	Even Difference Grey Model (EDGM)	The model is applicable when the analysed data sequence satisfies the assumptions of an approximate homogeneous exponential series, fluctuating sequence. The model can also be applied when the data meet the assumptions of a homogeneous exponential sequence. Therefore, it can be an alternative to the ODGM model	Liu et al. [13, 14]
	Discrete Grey Model (DGM)	This model has an application area identical to the EDGM model. Its relevance is mainly theoretical, since its construction solves the problem of transformation from discrete to continuous form in GM(1,1) class models	Xie et al. [15]

(continued)

Table 4.3 (continued)

Type	Model name	Areas of application of the model	Source/author
	Fractional Order Discrete Model (FODM)	This model is applicable when dealing with a sequence with memory and genetic characteristics. The model uses the fractional order cumulative operator in data preprocessing. The model allows the relationship between the significance of earlier data and more recent data in a time series to be taken into account	Wu et al. [16]
	Self-Meemory Pediction Grey Model (SMGM)	The model adopts the self-memory principle of dynamic systems, which is the basis for the integration of random and deterministic approaches in forecasting	Pei et al. [5]
Group models $GM(\mathrm{r, h})$	Classic model $GM(\mathrm{r, h})$ $(r \in N; h \in N)$	General form for all GM models. Depending on the parameters r i h the model can have different properties. The model has theoretical relevance. This form of the GM model has theoretical and cognitive significance for formal generalisations	Li et al. [17]
	Model $GM(0, \mathrm{N})$ $(r = 0; h = N)$	This is a static model with no derivatives. It is applicable when we have many factors influencing the predicted variable. This model can be an alternative to statistical regression models when the number of data is small	Li et al. [17]
	Multivariable Discrete Grey Model (MDGM)	Discrete form of the classical model $GM(\mathrm{r, h})$. This form of the GM model has theoretical and cognitive relevance for formal generalisations	Zhang [18]
	Drive Control Multivariable Discrete Grey Model (DCDGM)	Dynamic model with multiple variables. This model not only makes it possible to accurately predict the states of the system but also to explain its mechanisms of operation and control	Zhang [18]
	Grey Verhulst Model (GVM) and model $GM(2, 1)$	These two models have an identical range of applications. They can be used when the predicted phenomenon can be approximated by a sigmoidal or s-shaped function	Deng [3, 4], Evans [19], Zhao and Chen [20]

approach to this issue proposed in the literature [21, 22], pp. 209–211; [23], pp. 275–277), let us assume that we have a given time sequence on which the predictive model was built:

$$X_0 = (x_0(1), x_0, \ldots, x_0(n))$$

Below, however, we have a sequence of data resulting from a simulation derived from the developed model.

$$\hat{X}_0 = (\widehat{x_0}(1), \widehat{x_0}(2), \ldots, \widehat{x_0}(n))$$

Using both data sequences, the model error sequences can be determined. The first characterises the absolute error and is determined as follows:

$$\varepsilon_0 = (\varepsilon_0(1), \varepsilon_0(2) \ldots \varepsilon_0(n)) = (x_0(1) - \widehat{x_0}(1), x_0(2) - \widehat{x_0}(2), \ldots, x_0(n) - \widehat{x_0}(n))$$

The second forecast error sequence, on the other hand, is relative in nature and is determined as follows.

$$\Delta = \left(\left| \frac{\varepsilon_0(1)}{x_0(1)} \right|, \left| \frac{\varepsilon_0(2)}{x_0(2)} \right|, \ldots, \left| \frac{\varepsilon_0(n)}{x_0(n)} \right| \right) = \{\Delta_i\}_1^n$$

Taking the designations introduced, the average relative model error can be determined.

$$\overline{\Delta} = \frac{1}{n} \sum_{i=1}^{n} \Delta_i$$

However, by determining the value of $1 - \overline{\Delta}$, we obtain the average relative accuracy.

The error measures shown are used to assess the quality of the forecasting model. The principle of their use can be reduced to the following rules:

- An arbitrarily acceptable prediction error for the researcher should be adopted α which should depend on its validity and the context of use, with the lower the value, the higher the quality requirements for the model.
- Then, if $\overline{\Delta} < \alpha$ and at each point $\Delta_i < \alpha$, then such a model should be considered positively verified.

Another way of assessing the quality of a forecasting model is to use the absolute of the grey incidence ε between X_0 and $\hat{X}_0$. We can reduce the principle of using this indicator to the following rules:

- There should be an arbitrarily acceptable indicator acceptable to the researcher ε_0, whose value should be no more than one; this indicator should depend on the validity and context of the forecast use, with the higher the value ε_0, the higher the requirements for the quality of the model.

- Then, if in value $\varepsilon > \varepsilon_{0,}$ Then such a model should be considered positively validated.

Using basic statistical measures, the root mean square deviation (RMSD) and small error probability (SEP) assessment models can also be determined. To determine these two models to evaluate the quality of GM, it is first necessary to determine the arithmetic mean ($\overline{x}$) and standard deviation (S_1^2) of the raw data series and the arithmetic mean ($\overline{\varepsilon}$) and standard deviation (S_2^2) of the data from the forecast error sequence ε_0:

$$\overline{x} = \frac{1}{n}\sum_{k=1}^{n} x_0(k)\ S_1^2 = \frac{1}{n}\sum_{k=1}^{n}(x_0(k) - \overline{x})^2$$
$$\overline{\varepsilon} = \frac{1}{n}\sum_{k=1}^{n} \varepsilon(k)\ S_2^2 = \frac{1}{n}\sum_{k=1}^{n}(\varepsilon(k) - \overline{\varepsilon})^2$$

In the RMSD model, the rules for assessing model quality can be reduced to the following rules:

- we calculate the coefficient $C = \frac{S_2}{S_1}$ and take an arbitrary value of $C_0 > 0$.
- then, if the value $C < C_{0,}$ Then the forecasting model should be considered positively validated.

However, in the case of SEPs, we apply the following rules of conduct:

- Calculate the probability p and check whether the following relationship holds: $p = P(\varepsilon(k) - \overline{\varepsilon}) < 0,6745S_1$ for each item k.
- If the above mentioned relationship holds, then we arbitrarily adopt the indicator $p_0 > 0$.
- If $p > p_0$, then such a predictive model should be considered positively validated.

In assessing the quality of forecasting models, an important function is played by arbitrarily adopted reference values α, ε_0, C_0, p_0 To facilitate this task, Table 4.4 can be used with four levels of accuracy [21, 22]. Given that in forecasting in a management context, the main task is to identify trends in the data, level III and IV can be accepted as sufficient for research in this area. However, the more the researcher cares about the accuracy of the estimation in time coordinates, the more he/she should choose Level I and Level II.

The evaluation of the model's accuracy estimate is a fundamental element of its systematic validation. If the model is positively validated for accuracy, then in the next stage its optimisation on new data is refinement, control, and optional. On the other hand, if the model has been negatively validated, then in the optimisation step it is necessary to acquire new data and re-estimate the model parameters on them in order to reach the assumed level of model quality. If this is not possible because successive iterative optimisations of the model do not yield positive verification, then a logical change to the model structure is required. It is then necessary to rethink its concept at the linguistic modelling level.

4.4 Guidelines for the Application of Grey Decision-Making Models

Decision models are a diverse and difficult to clearly classify group of models in grey systems theory. Moreover, they have many alternatives that do not use concepts derived from GST. It should be emphasised that the guidelines for their selection and application will mainly be driven by assumptions from typical decision-making processes. To a small extent, they will be specific only to the decision-making methods proposed in the GST. In detail, the model selection process will follow the algorithm shown in Fig. 4.4.

The first stage in the decision-making model selection procedure is the stage whose purpose is to identify the decision problem. A decision problem is a situation in which the decision-maker, or decision-maker, must choose an action from a set of at least two of its options or refrain consciously and deliberately from any action [24], pp. 44–45. In another perspective, by decision-making, we can define the process of choosing a given variant of action, caused by the adopted criteria of their valuation.

The set of decision options should be the starting point for the algorithm to select an appropriate decision model. In grey systems theory, this set forms a decision space determined by the Cartesian product of two sets. The first is the set of events that exhaust the relevant states of the object against which the decision is made. The second, on the other hand, is the set of measures that can significantly affect the characteristics of the states of the object in question. To express this formally, let us assume that the set of A is the set of events, while the set B—the set of countermeasures [21], pp. 227–229:

$$A = \{a_1, a_2, \ldots, a_n\}, \text{ where}: \ a_i \text{ is } i - \text{this event}, \ i = 1, 2, \ldots n$$
$$B = \{b_1, b_2, \ldots, b_m\}, \text{ where}: b_i \text{ is } i \ - \text{this measure}, \ i = 1, 2, \ldots m$$

Table 4.4 Values of reference indicators to test the accuracy of predictive models

Level of precision	Relative error (α)	Degree of incidence (ε_0)	Variance ratio (C_0)	Small error probability (p_0)
I	0.01	0.90	0.35	0.95
II	0.05	0.80	0.50	0.80
III	0.10	0.70	0.65	0.70
IV	0.20	0.60	0.80	0.60

Source Liu et al. [21], p. 211

Taking this designation, the set of decision options can be written as follows.

$$A \times B = \{ (a_i, b_j) | a_i \in A, b_i \in B\}$$

Assuming that $s_{ij} = (a_i, b_j)$ for each $a_i \in A, b_i \in B$, then the set $S = A \times B$ we can call the set of options or decision schemes.

Once the decision problem has been identified and the decision options have been identified, the next step in selecting a decision model is to identify the structure of the decision problem. This structure should show the relationship between the following elements: set of decision options, decision subject, decision criteria, formal tools for modelling information in the decision process. As mentioned earlier, the set of decision options is determined by the combination of countermeasures in relation to the states of the decision object. The object, or otherwise sometimes referred to as the decision object, in the structure of a decision problem is therefore reflected and analysed in terms of the generation of decision options. The subject of the decision, on the other hand, is the person or set of persons with the power to select a decision option and the authority to implement it. If the subject of the decision only has the power of opinion and no authority to transform the decision into action, in that case, we can speak of a decision support process. Another element in the structure of the decision problem is the set of criteria for making the decision. This is the element that determines that the decision-making process seeks to target actions. Therefore, a well-constructed set of criteria should provide a guarantee of

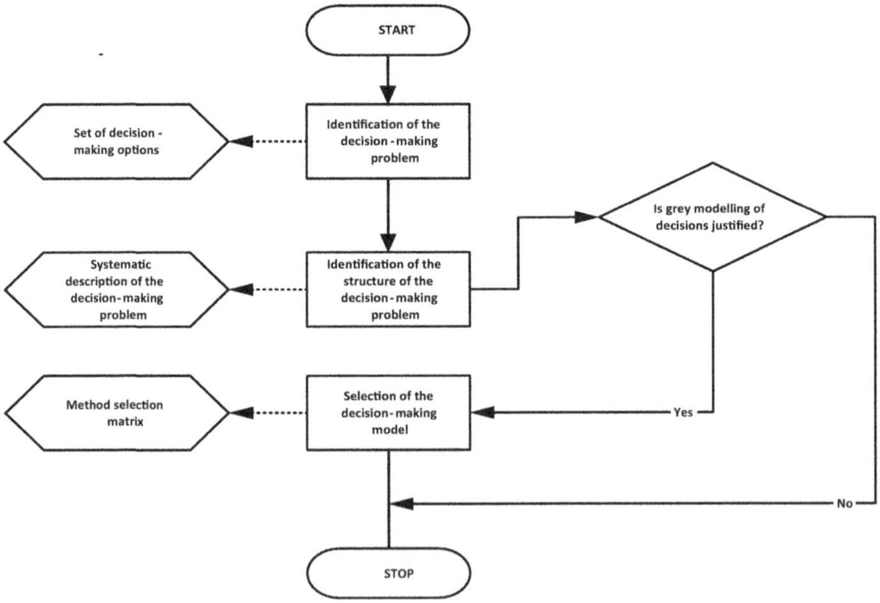

Fig. 4.4 Procedure to proceed with the research process using grey decision models

transparency in the decision-making process and should eliminate its arbitrariness to the maximum extent. The last element of the structure of the decision-making problem can collectively be called the formal tools of information modelling in the decision-making process. These tools are nothing more than a set of methods by which information can be described and then transformed and interpreted in quantitative terms. If the set of tools includes methods based on basic grey theoretical constructs such as grey numbers, whitening functions, or the distributive interpretation of grey, we call such models grey decision-making models. An exhaustive description of the decision structure must be framed systemically. This systemicity can be modelled purely formally on models, as is most commonly found in the literature [21–23], or it can be shown ideatively on the basis of diagrams. The latter way is more conceptually transparent and hence recommended in the context of management research [25]. With knowledge of the structure of the decision problem, an important point of consideration is to answer the question of whether grey modelling is valid. To do so, it is necessary to consider the form of information available to us in the decision-making process. If this information is uncertain in the sense that grey decision-making constructs are applicable to its modelling, then the answer is positive. Another case in favour of using grey decision models may be their fit to the structure of the decision problem. The idea here is that, by virtue of the principle of economy of operation, the grey approach is chosen because it requires the least number of transformations and assumptions about the raw data generated in the context of the individual elements of the decision-problem structure. In terms of answering the question of validity, the findings on the demarcation criteria between grey systems theory and fuzzy and probabilistic approaches should also be in force. Once the question of validity has been answered positively, the next step is to select an appropriate model. In this regard, the decision method selection matrix shown in Table 4.5 should be used.

The selection of a decision model using the matrix shown in Table 4.5 should take into account, on the one hand, the structure of the decision problem and, on the other hand, two aspects: the form in which the expression of grey in the problem takes place and the decision perspective.

Regarding the form of grey, if the information needed for decision making is expressed through grey numbers, then the range of models will be limited to GND and GNCD only. On the contrary, when we have grey information that can be interpreted distributively, the number of models is much larger and more diverse. However, it is then more difficult for studies to carry out a proof of principle for the use of the grey approach, because the demarcation between methods based on a distributive understanding of grey and other decision-making models is theoretically sublime. In contrast, models based on a whitening function are burdened with a high level of subjectivity because of the arbitrariness of the form of the whitening function. Another problem is also that whitening functions should not be confused with membership functions in fuzzy logic. These are two incompatible constructs from a different theoretical approach. They may have similarities; however, their interpretation and meaning in modelling are different.

Table 4.5 Selection matrix for decision-making methods

Model name	Structure of a characteristic decision-making problem	Comments on the model	Type of grey			Decision-making perspective		
			GN	WF	DG	L1	L2	L3
Grey Target Decisions (GTD) [21–23, 25, 27]	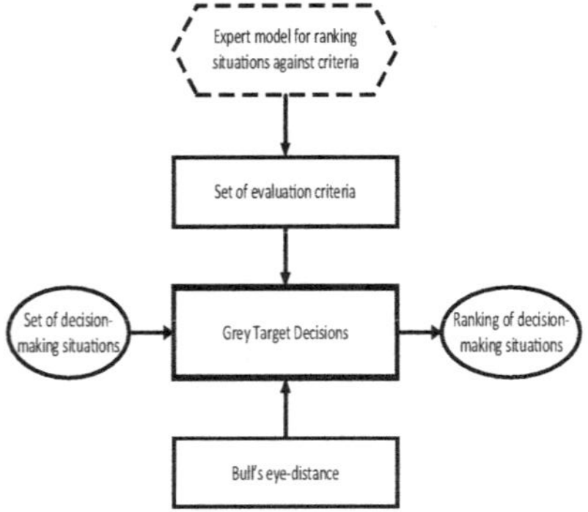	We use the model when the decision-maker's objectives have a high degree of freedom. The model may or may not use expert estimates. It can be designed to use objective and formal quantitative criteria	×	×	√	×	×	√
Grey Incidence Decisions (GID) [5, 21–23, 28]		We use this model in similar cases to the GTD model. This model also includes the option of expert ranking of decision situations. Furthermore, due to the use of GIA in the calculation procedures, it is possible to introduce the concept of expressing the importance of individual decision criteria	×	×	√	×	×	√

(continued)

Table 4.5 (continued)

Model name	Structure of a characteristic decision-making problem	Comments on the model	Type of grey			Decision-making perspective		
			GN	WF	DG	L1	L2	L3
Grey Numbers Decisions (GND) [17]	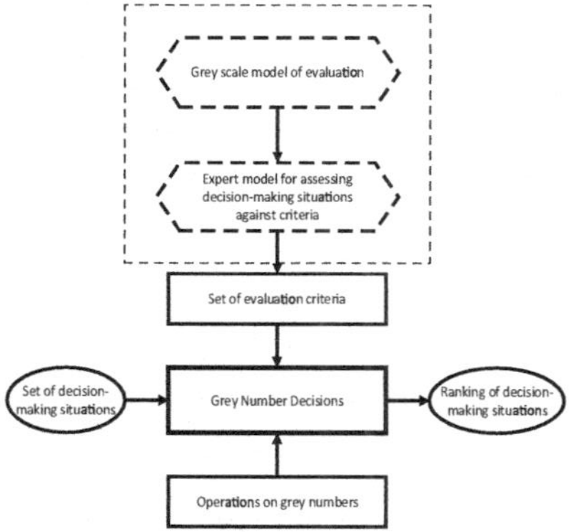	The model is primarily an expert model to evaluate decision options based on the adopted criteria. Formally, it is possible to select the criteria in such a way as to avoid expert judgements; however, this is not used. In some cases, the model may have difficulties in strictly ranking all the options. However, it makes it possible to always identify the most important option. The model can also vary the weights of the decision criteria	√	×	×	×	×	√
Grey Numbers Clustering Decisions (GNCD) [25, 29]		It is similar to the GND model. It is a modification of it. This model does not rank objects, but assigns objects to predefined groups. The number of these groups is maximally determined by the number of states on the evaluation scale. It is always one less than the number of scale states. This model can be transformed into an evaluation model. In this model, the decision criteria can also be weighted	√	×	×	×	×	√

(continued)

Table 4.5 (continued)

Model name	Structure of a characteristic decision-making problem	Comments on the model	Type of grey			Decision-making perspective		
			GN	WF	DG	L1	L2	L3
Grey Feedback Loop Decisions (GFLD) [25]	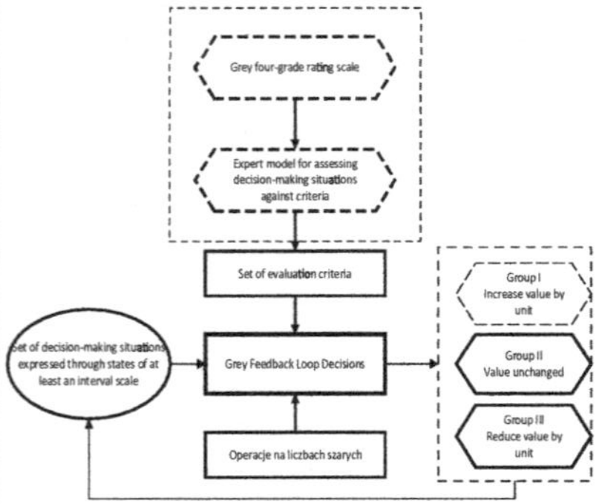	The model assumes that the set of decision situations will be mapped using at least an *interval scale*. In the model, experts assess whether a given current decision situation should be unchanged, should change, such that the value assigned to it increases by a unit, or whether, on the contrary, it should decrease by the adopted unit This is a model that exhibits the characteristics of a control model. The assessment of options in this model is limited to a grey scale of a four-point mapping scale. Criteria can be weighted in the model	√	×	×	×	×	√
Grey Development Decisions (GDD) [23]		The model takes into account the development trends that affect the decision-making situation. The decision is made on the basis of a forecast. The model is anticipatory in nature. It takes into account future developments more than the current state	×	×	√	×	√	×

(continued)

Table 4.5 (continued)

Model name	Structure of a characteristic decision-making problem	Comments on the model	Type of grey			Decision-making perspective		
			GN	WF	DG	L1	L2	L3
Grey Statistical Decision (GSD) [23, 30, 31]	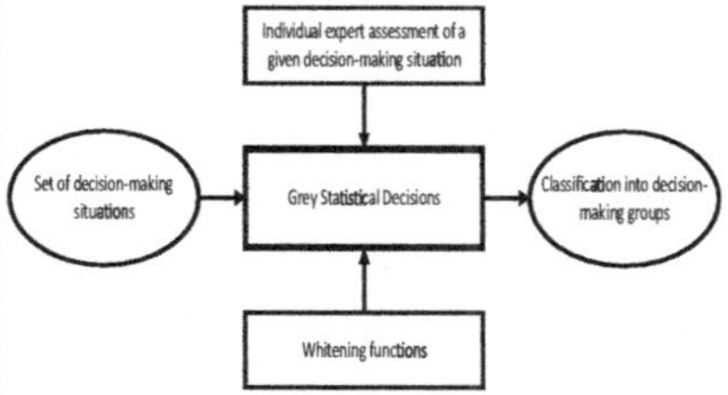	This model does not use decision criteria. The evaluation of decision options is carried out by a group of experts for the option as a whole. Each expert evaluates an option individually. The model is useful for decision-making by large groups of people with relatively small and fuzzy levels of responsibility for their decisions. The model is therefore suitable for the preliminary identification of the preferences of large groups of stakeholders. The model can be easily transposed into an evaluation model	×	√	×	√	×	×
Grey Cluster Decisions (GCD) [23, 32]	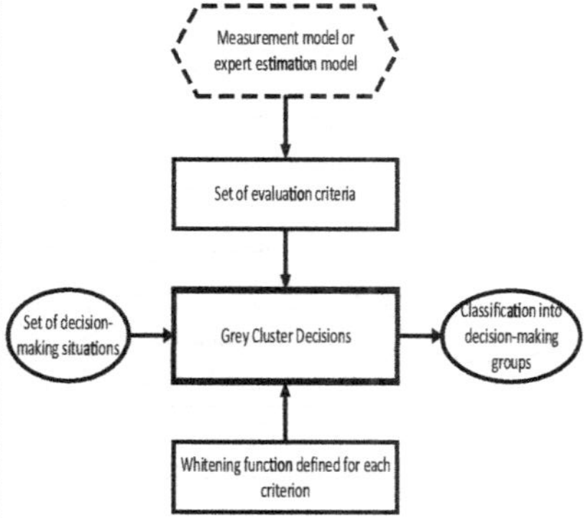	The model is based on a baseline whitening function defined for each criterion. Criteria can be weighted. The model requires the construction of a measurement model for each decision situation against each criterion. An expert estimation model may also be used. It is important that expert and measurement-based approaches can be combined in the model. The model can be easily transformed into an evaluation model	×	√	×	×	×	√

(continued)

Table 4.5 (continued)

Model name	Structure of a characteristic decision-making problem	Comments on the model	Type of grey			Decision-making perspective		
			GN	WF	DG	L1	L2	L3
Multiple-Target-Situation Decisions with Synthesized Target (MTSDST) [23, 33, 34]	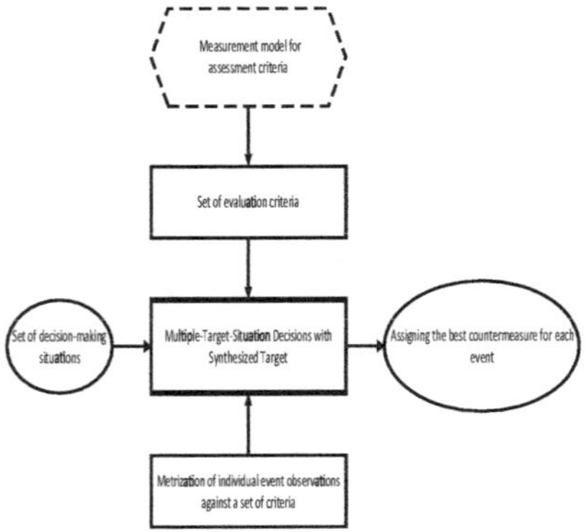	This model uses metrication principles to normalise decision criteria. These criteria can be treated as stimulants, destimulants, or optima. The criteria of the model can be weighted. The model assigns the best countermeasure for each event. It can therefore be used in all solution selection problems where a change in the state of the environment requires a reaction as to the courses of action. Allows the space of possible behaviours to be analysed. In this way, it is useful for generating management scenarios	×	×	√	×	×	√
Grey-Stratified Decisions (GSTD) [23, 35, 36]		This model integrates other decision-making models. It allows the perspectives of different stakeholders to be taken into account and balanced in the decision-making process. Each stakeholder group is classified into a decision-making layer for which a corresponding disaster-making model is addressed. For the mass layer, this is the GSD model, for the expert layer the GDC, and for the administrative layer the GCD	×	√	√	√	√	√

Legend: GN—grey number, WF—whitening function, DG—distributive grey understanding; L1—methods for the mass decision maker, L1—methods for the expert decision maker, L3—method for the administrative decision maker

With regard to the second aspect, the decision-making perspective, this issue is described in detail in Sect. 2.4. It should only be added that the assignment to the individual perspectives shown in Table 4.5 is not definitive. Only shows in which layer the model fits best. This should be taken into account when several models fit into the structure of the decision problem. Then it can be the decisive criterion. However, this does not change the fact that it is possible, although not optimal, to apply a given model in the context of a different perspective than the developed method selection matrix.

An important issue in the field of decision-making models, and this does not only apply to grey models, is their relation to evaluative or taxonomic models. In many cases, they have an identical formal mathematical structure. In GST, this problem is not addressed. Thus, there are evaluation and clustering models. They have their own nomenclature, different notation, however, on a formal level they are the same as decision models. Therefore, it can be concluded that these models are a specific case of decision-making models. The specificity of the evaluation and classification models in relation to the decision-making models is shown in Table 4.6.

Analysing the comparison shown in Table 4.6, we can make the following theses with respect to the GST:

- Decision models can easily be transformed into evaluation and classification models by reinterpreting the primary purpose of their use by the entity that applies them.
- Decision models are the starting point for evaluation models.
- Transforming a decision model into an evaluative or classification model requires abandoning the analytical Cartesian product approach to the decision space in favour of a more general notion of object.
- Any decision model that results in a classification of decision situations or a classification into value-ordered decision groups can be transformed into an evaluation model.
- Any decision model that results in a classification into value-ordered decision groups can be transformed into a classification model.

Evaluation and classification models are undoubtedly at a logical level but also historically derivative of decision models. Historically, they appeared later than decision models. In the classical range of considerations at the very beginning of GST, they were overlooked [37]. However, the further development of GST and utilitarian and practical considerations led to the development of evaluation and classification models based on decision solutions [38, 39]. Hence, in research processes, if an evaluation or classification model is needed, one needs to use Table 4.6. and select the appropriate model for the problem. Then it needs to be transformed into a classification or evaluation model. The second way is to use ready-made solutions available in the literature, where such a transformation has already been done. A collection of canonical models of this type together with a description is shown in Table 4.7.

As can be seen in Tables 4.6 and 4.7, the issues of decision making and classification and evaluation overlap. Many differences can of course be identified, however, adopting the criterion of mathematical formalism, the issue is very similar. However,

Table 4.6 Comparison of the decision-making model with an evaluation or classification model

Comparison criterion	Decision-making model	Evaluation model	Classification model
Objectives	The purpose is to assist the decision-making process of the decision maker. The objective is utilitarian, a better choice from a range of options at a given time and place and under given conditions	The objective is to value the particular object being evaluated. The purpose is cognitive or diagnostic. Only the results of the evaluation can be used to make decisions or shape policies and strategies	The aim is to classify the given objects into groups. These groups should contain objects that are indistinguishable in terms of the classification characteristics adopted. The groups may or may not be in a value order. The classification is mainly cognitive in nature
Entity	A person or group of people with varying degrees of responsibility for the consequences of decisions. They usually have an opinion-making voice. However, they may also be an entity that can implement the decision. Depending on the authority of the entity, we speak of a decision-making process or a decision-support process	A person or group of persons whose aim is to know and order objects separated from reality. The manner of this ordering will result from the structure of the needs of the subject so identified, It will be manifested in the criteria of evaluation	A person or group of persons whose aim is to organise into homogeneous groups the objects to be classified
Subject	The decision situation is the product of a Cartesian set of events and a set of countermeasures	An evaluation object understood as a discrete piece of reality subject to analysis	A classification object understood as a discrete piece of reality subject to analysis
Formal tools for information provision	Grey numbers, models based on a distributive understanding of grey, whitening functions	Grey numbers, models based on a distributive understanding of grey, whitening functions	Grey numbers, models based on a distributive understanding of grey, whitening functions
Result	Selection of the best decision situation or, in the case of the MTSDST model, the best countermeasure for each decision option	Ranking of objects or the assignment of objects to groups ordered according to an accepted valuation criterion	Assignment of objects to groups. Groups may or may not be value-ordered

Table 4.7 Characteristics of canonical evaluation and classification models

Model name	Model characteristics	Model type
Grey incidence clustering model	This model classifies objects into groups based on the similarity index of objects determined by GIA methods. This model requires observation of the criteria in the survey sample. Thus, any caveats about GIA models also apply to this model. The model is the grey equivalent of cluster analysis	Classification model with groups of values ordered
Variable weight grey clustering model	Classification model based on a whitening function. The model assumes that the classification criteria will have the same unit of measurement. At a formal level, the model is derived from the GCD model	A classification model with value-ordered groups. The model can, therefore, be an evaluation model
Fixed weight grey clustering model	This model differs from the Variable Weight Grey Clustering Model in that the classification criteria can have different units of measurement. At a formal level, this model is also derived from the GCD model	A classification model with value-ordered groups. The model can be an evaluation model
Grey clustering evaluation models based on mixed possibility functions	The model allows classification into value-ordered groups using standard whitening functions. The standard form of these functions has been developed in two versions. These can be functions based on the concept of central-point triangular possibility functions [8] or on the concept of end-point mixed possibility function [13, 14]	A classification model with value-ordered groups. The model is also an evaluation model

from the point of view of applications in management science research, there may be differences summarised in Table 4.6. However, despite their existence, it should be stated that the general way of proceeding for decision-making, evaluation, and classification models is similar and can be reduced to the algorithm shown in Fig. 4.3 with minor adjustments. However, the logic and order are the same. Therefore, it made sense to show the decision-making models first and then indicate general directions for their modification and transformation in terms of evaluation or classification.

4.5 Guidelines for the Application of Grey Hybrid Models

Grey hybrid models are the result of the integration of classical generally known methods used in modelling management research problems with GST methods. Given the discernment made in the literature in Chap. 3, it can be assumed that, in the context of research in the management sciences, GST methods are mainly intended to extend the capabilities of other methodological approaches. In the research in question, they are usually the underlying models. To accurately describe the relationships that occur between methods in the process of their integration, an approach based on the system integration known in action systems engineering was proposed by [40]. Let us therefore assume that each research method is a system of teleologically ordered activities and that the relationship between methods can be considered in terms of three criteria: superiority, position in relation to each other, and openness to external information.

The first is the criterion of superiority. It makes it possible to determine which method is the base method and constitutes the germ of the integrated method, and to indicate which method constitutes the auxiliary method. The base method is the method whose main objectives are taken over by the integrated method. The auxiliary method, on the other hand, extends the analytical capabilities of the base method. Graphically, this can be written in the convention shown in Fig. 4.5.

The second criterion by which the relationship between methods can be shown is that of position in relation to each other. Here, we can distinguish a relationship in which one method feeds information to another method. This method is then called a hedging method, whereas a method that uses the results of another method as input is called an operational method. This is shown illustratively in Fig. 4.6a and b. Figure 4.6a shows a situation where the base method is also an operational method and the auxiliary method is a hedging method. On the contrary, in Fig. 4.6b, the base method is the security method, and the auxiliary method is the operational method.

A third criterion by which we can examine the relationship between integrated methods is that of openness to external information. In this case, we can distinguish between an open integrated method, where the combined methods use data from multiple inputs in their information flows and can generate information through more than just one output. On the other hand, a closed integrated method only uses data from one input and only generates results for one output. Graphically showing whether a method is open- or closed-type can be mapped by introducing additional inputs and outputs. However, at the same time, the diagram must clearly show what

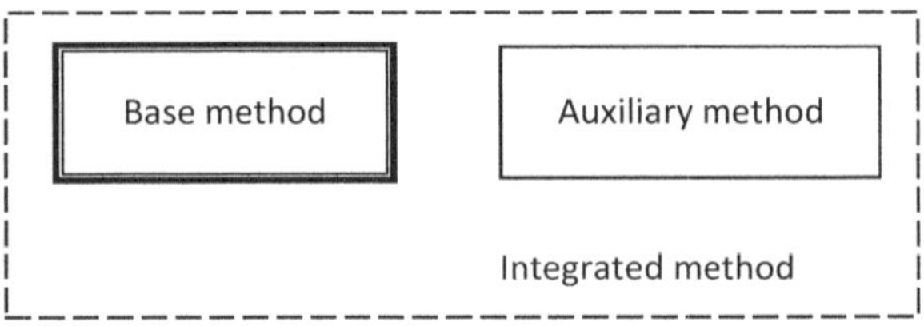

Fig. 4.5 Graphical convention for recording the relationship between methods based on the criterion of superiority

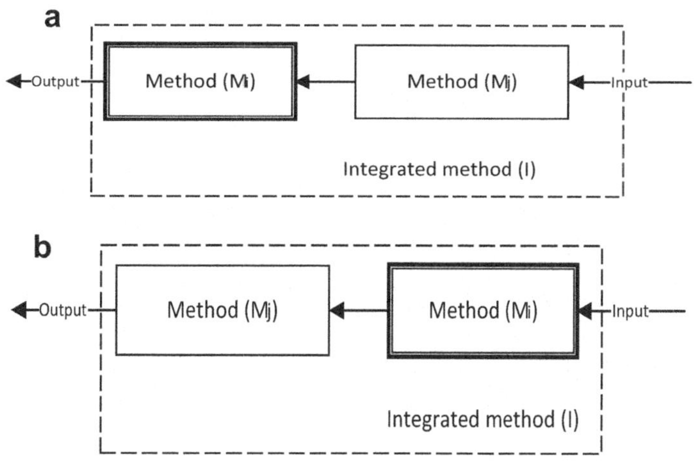

Fig. 4.6 Security of the base method by the auxiliary method, **b** Security of the auxiliary method by the base method

is the main input and what is the main output of the integrated method. This can be done by reserving straight horizontal arrows on the diagrams for these types of input, while drawing other inputs and outputs vertically from above or below with arrows with broken lines. Another way is to verbally or graphically bold the main input and output.

The three analysis criteria for the situation between the two methods subject to integration are shown above. In this way, the categories for describing integration relationships, which are the building blocks for more complex group cases, are discussed in a two-element context. The three analysis criteria discussed give rise to the formulation of elementary types of integration between the two methods. These types are discussed in Table 4.8. For each type, a diagram is shown, a symbolic notation is provided, and comments are made in relation to the management research issue. In the table, the grey methods are assumed to be auxiliary methods.

Given the characteristics of the different integration types and the resulting possibilities for creating grey hybrid methods, this process can be expressed in a more structured way in the form of an algorithm for identifying and selecting integration types in grey hybrid methods. Such an algorithm is shown in Fig. 4.7.

Summarising the issue of grey hybrid research methods and synthesising the information in Table 4.8 and the algorithm guidelines in Fig. 4.7, it is reasonable to formulate the following rules for the application of grey hybrid models in management research.

1. The starting point in the application of grey hybrid methods is the identification of uncertain information at the input or output of the underlying analytical method in a given research process, which can be formalised by theoretical constructs derived from the theory associated with the grey space.

Table 4.8 Types of method integration in the context of grey hybrid methods

Type	Diagram	Token entry	Comments
Operational integration closed	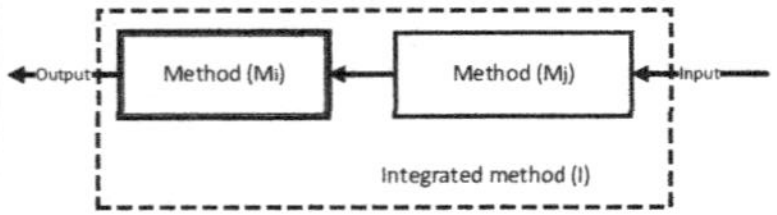	$I =< M_i; M_j >$ M_i—base method M_j—grey method as an auxiliary method	The hybrid method resulting from the operational integration of a simple method is valid only for research applications *when representative empirical material* is available. The representativeness of the input data must, therefore, be clearly justified in the research process. However, it should be noted that other characteristics of the data should indicate the validity of using Grey methods. An example of this type of method is Grey-DEMATEL which has found a wide range of applications in management (cf. Table 3.3). This method is an example of the integration of grey number arithmetic and classical DEMATEL. The DEMATEL in this arrangement is the basis for the integrated method
Operational integration is open	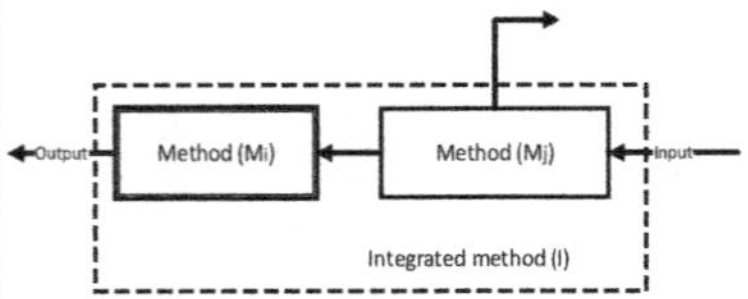	$I =< M_i; (M_j) >$ M_i—base method (M_j)—grey method as an auxiliary method with an additional side output	The hybrid method, which is the result of open operational integration, is similar in application to the methods resulting from closed operational integration. The only difference is that the method M_j in addition to feeding the results of the method M_i can be used to carry out side research, relative to the main objective. An example of this type of research using a grey hybrid method could be the integration of the DEMATEL method and the GIA method [41]. In addition to determining the strength of the relationship using the DEMATEL method, the GIA model can also be used for additional analyses, such as factor clustering for the construction of evaluation indices

(continued)

Table 4.8 (continued)

Type	Diagram	Token entry	Comments
Security integration closed	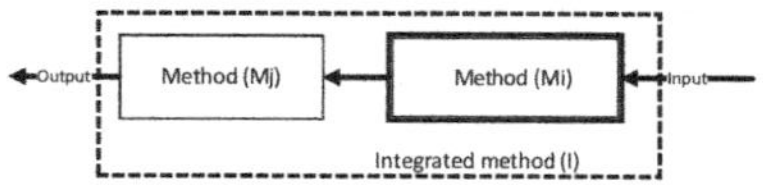	$I =< M_j; M_i >$ M_i—base method M_j—grey method as an auxiliary method	The hybrid method, which is the result of closed-loop hedging integration, can be used when additional relationships between results are required to be captured, greater precision of results is required, or studies in predictive mode, i.e., for specific results from the method M_i their prediction for subsequent time units. It is important that the input data are rigorously prepared in terms of representativeness. An example of a study using a closed-form hedge integration approach is one in which the AHP method was integrated with a GRA model [42, 43]
Security integration open	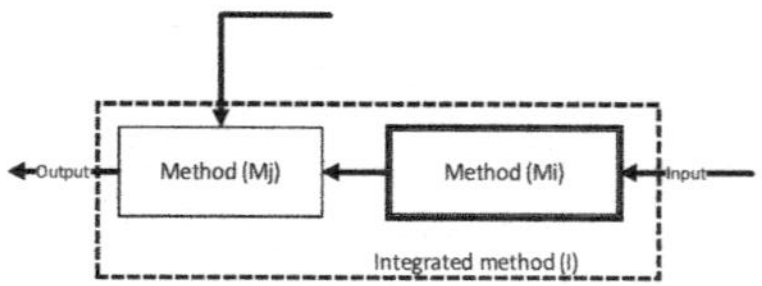	$I =< (M_j); M_i >$ M_i—base method (M_j)—grey method as an auxiliary method with an additional side input	The hybrid method resulting from open safety integration has a similar range of research applications to closed safety integration. The difference is that by feeding the method with M_j data, it is possible to triangulate methods or data easily. In this case, the approach may be beneficial when there are legitimate concerns that the empirical material does not fully meet the rigours of representativeness. This type of integration is postulated. It is very difficult to find in the literature a hybrid method resulting from this type of integration. An example, usually not fully realising this model of integration, can be observed in the case of complex decision-making methods [44]

(continued)

Table 4.8 (continued)

Type	Diagram	Token entry	Comments
Feedback integration closed	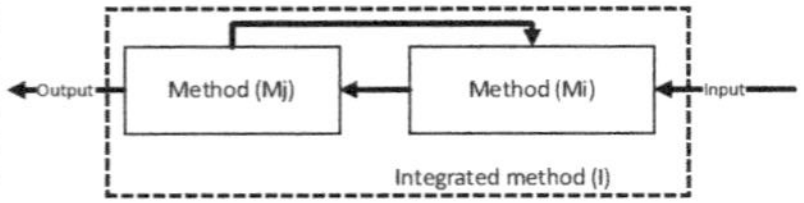	$I = \ll M_j;\ M_i >;$ $< M_i;\ M_j \gg$ M_i; M_j—equivalent research methods in an operational-security relationship (the position of the methods is irrelevant) Formally, we can write the equivalence as follows $M_i \equiv M_j$	The hybrid method resulting from closed-loop feedback integration is used when the parameters of individual methods need to be adaptively adjusted. It is especially relevant in the reliability assessment process of predictive models, where the GM(1,1) model is coupled with the root mean square deviation (RMSD) and small error probability (SEP) assessment models (see: 4.3. and [21, 22], pp. 209–211; [23], pp. 275–277)
Open feedback integration	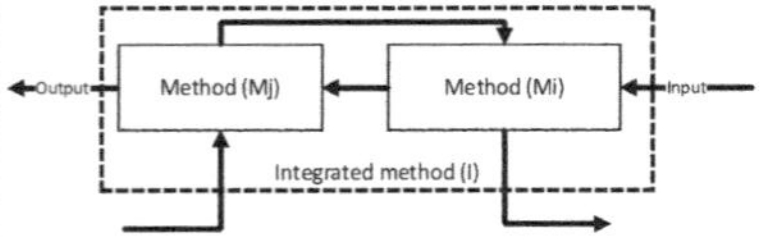	$I = \ll (M_j);\ (M_i) >;$ $< (M_i);\ (M_j) \gg$ (M_i); (M_j)—equivalent research methods in an operational-security relationship Formally, we can write the equivalence as follows $(M_i) \equiv (M_j)$	The hybrid method resulting from open-ended feedback integration has the same scope of application as closed-ended integration. The difference is that the results should be triangulated; they allow for side objectives to the main objective of the study. The model is postulative. No application is described in the literature

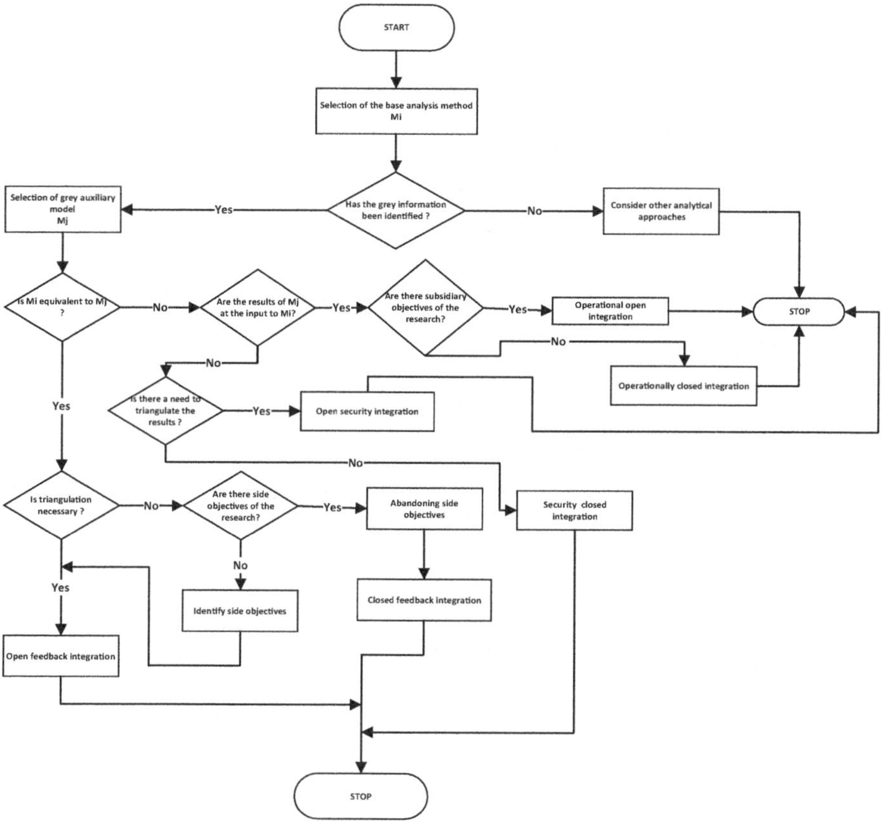

Fig. 4.7 Model for identification and selection of integration type in the construction of grey hybrid models

2. In line with the current state of knowledge contained in the literature, the grey research approach is an auxiliary approach in the field of management research. This has a historical and logical rationale since, relative to other approaches such as statistical methods, fuzzy logic, or rough set theory, grey systems theory is a relatively young field of knowledge with a less established research tradition and popularity. This argument may seem irrelevant from the point of view of the methodology proposed by Popper; however, considering the sociological aspects of scientific research in terms of Kuhn's paradigms or Lakatos' research programmes, it becomes pan-rational and legitimate.
3. When integrating two equivalent methods, i.e. when$M_i \equiv M_j$, we are dealing with operational-security feedback integration. Methods resulting from this type of integration are used when dynamic phenomena are being studied, and the formal parameters of a method or model need to be continuously adjusted and adapted. These models can be open or closed. An open model allows for side objectives and requires the implementation of a triangulation procedure. The lack

of triangulation should mean abandoning methods based on open-ended feedback integration $I = \ll M_j; M_i >; < M_i; M_j \gg$, in favour of methods resulting from closed feedback integration: $I = \ll (M_j); (M_i) >; < (M_i); (M_j) \gg$.

- Grey methods can occupy a hedging position or an operational position. An operational position is when the results of a grey method M_j constitute an input to the underlying method M_i. The reverse is indicative of operational integration. There is no indication of a preference for either position. It is only important to emphasise the fact that, in the current state of the literature, the most popular grey hybrid method used in management, Grey-DEMATEL, is the result of closed operational integration.
- In the cases where the grey method feeds into the baseline method and we have data that meet the rigour of representativeness, it is worth considering setting additional side objectives for the survey and thus developing a method based on the operational integration of open $I = <M_i; (M_j)>$. If there is no need for secondary objectives and a high level of data representativeness, we design and apply a method based on *closed* operational integration $I = <M_i; (M_j)>$.
- Where there is a situation in which the grey method M_j is fed with information by the base method M_i we then speak of security integration. This can be open or closed. The methods resulting from closed integration $I = <M_i; (M_j)>$ are used when we want to increase the precision of the results of the base method or when we want to extrapolate them to subsequent time units. It is important that the input data meet the rigours of representativeness. When such representativeness is lacking, the results should be made plausible by means of triangulation. This method will then be constructed according to an open-ended hedge integration scheme.

Because hybrid methods can be generated from other methods unrelated to grey systems theory, their analysis in the context of research applications is hindered by their great diversity. For descriptive purposes, for the use of literature research, the characterisation of the integration that takes place in hybrid methods can be based on the cybernetic concept of preprocessing, processing, or postprocessing. It has a focus on the description of the component methods, taking into account only the criterion of position in them. In the case of research process design, on the other hand, it does not provide a coherent description of the issue and a sufficient basis for formulating general principles and selecting the structure of hybrid methods. The adopted practical convention based on theory and action engineering captures this aspect of the issue without losing the qualities of generality. At a methodological level, it provides a coherent and flexible theoretical framework through which new hybrid methods can be analysed and designed. They can have a more complex structure, generated on a composite of basic integration types. Thus, they can be better adapted to the characteristics of a given research or practice problem.

References

1. Azam, M.S.: The diffusion of ICT and SME performance. In: Quaddus, M., Woodside, A.G. (eds.) Advances in Business Marketing and Purchasing, pp. 7–290. Bingley, Emerald Group Publishing Limited (2015)
2. Zott, C., Amit, R.: Business model design: an activity system perspective. Long Range Plan. **43**, 216–226 (2010)
3. Deng, J.L.: Grey System Control. Huazhong University of Science and Technology Press, Wuhan (1985)
4. Deng, J.: Grey Control System. Printing House of Central China University of Science and Technology, Hubei (1985)
5. Pei, L.-l., Chen, W.-M., Cui, J.-F., Zhuang, G.-B.: Weighted degree of grey incidence based on optimization entropy. In: IEEE International Conference on Grey Systems and Intelligent Services, GSIS 2009, Nanjing, pp. 340–343
6. Zhang, Q.S., Guo, X.J., Deng, J.L.: Grey relation entropy method of grey relation analysis. Syst. Eng. Theory Pract. **8**, 7–11 (1996)
7. Liu, S., Guo, T.B.: Grey Systems Theory and Applications. Henan University Press, Kaifeng (1991)
8. Liu, S.F., Xie, N.M.: New grey evaluation method based on reformative triangular whitenization weight function. J. Syst. Eng. **26**, 244–250 (2011)
9. Honghua, W., Lixia, D., Hui, L.: *A New Grey Relational Degree Model for Panel Data and its Application.* Hangzhou, IEEE (2015)
10. Xie, N.: Explanations about grey information and framework of grey system modeling. Grey Syst.: Theory Appl. **7**, 179–193 (2017)
11. Xie, N.: A summary of grey forecasting models. Grey Syst.: Theory Appl. **12**, 703–722 (2022)
12. Deng, J.: Control problems of grey systems. Syst. Control Lett. **1**, 288–294 (1982)
13. Liu, S., Yang, Y., Fang, Z.-G., Xie, N.: Grey cluster evaluation models based on mixed triangular whitenization weight functions. Grey Syst.: Theory Appl. **5**, 410–418 (2015)
14. Liu, S., et al.: Four basic models of GM (1, 1) and their suitable sequences. Grey Syst.: Theory Appl. **5**, 141–156 (2015)
15. Xie, N., Sifeng, L., Naiming, X., Sifeng, L.: *Research on Discrete Grey Model and Its Mechanism.* IEEE (2005)
16. Wu, L., Liu, S., Yao, L., Yan, S., Liu, D.: Grey system model with the fractional order accumulation. Commun. Nonlinear Sci. Numer. Simulat. **18**, 1775–1785 (2013)
17. Li, G.-D., Yamaguchi, D., Nagai, M.: A grey-based decision-making approach to the supplier selection problem. Math. Comput. Model. **46**, 573–581 (2007)
18. Zhang, K.: Multi-variables discrete grey model based on driver control. Syst. Eng.-Theory Pract. **34**, 2084–2091 (2014)
19. Evans, M.: An alternative approach to estimating the parameters of a generalised Grey Verhulst model: an application to steel intensity of use in the UK. Expert Syst. Appl. **41**, 1236–1244 (2014)
20. Zhao, X.Q., Chen, H.L.: Prediction formula's defect of GM (2, 1) and its improvement. J. Wuhan Univ. Technol. **28**, 125–131 (2006)
21. Liu, S., Yang, Y., Forrest, J.: *Grey Data Analysis.* Springer, Berlin (2017)
22. Liu, S., Zhang, H., Yang, Y.: Explanation of terms of grey incidence analysis models. Grey Syst.: Theory Appl. (2017)
23. Liu, S., Lin, Y.: *Grey Information: Theory and Practical Applications.* Springer Science & Business Media (2006)
24. Pszczołowski, T.: *The Little Enyckolpedia of Praxeology and Organisational Theory (in Polish).* Ossolineum, Wrocław (1978)
25. Mierzwiak, R., Nowak, M.: *Decision-making Models in Grey Systems Theory (in Polish).* PTE Poznań, Poznań (2020)

26. Liu, S.: *Multi-attribute intelligent grey target decision model.* In: ISTASC'10: Proceedings of the 10th WSEAS International Conference on Systems Theory and Scientific Computation. Taipei Taiwan, pp. 15–16 (2010)
27. Guo, S., Li, Q., Jing, Y., Guan, L.: A review of grey target decision model. J. Grey Syst. **34** (2022)
28. Quan, J., Zeng, B., Liu, D.: Green supplier selection for process industries using weighted grey incidence decision model. Complexity (2018)
29. Nowak, M., Borowiec, A.: Intuitive solution of decision-making problems using the grey systems theory. Organ. Rev. 28–35 (2019)
30. Gao, W.: Grey Statistical Decision Making for Estimate of the Regional Wheat Trials Yield. Atlantis Press, Xi'an (2018)
31. Liu, S., Yang, Y.: Explanation of terms of grey clustering evaluation models. Grey Syst.: Theory Appl **7**, 129–135 (2017)
32. Yu, J., Wang, D., Hu, C.: Selection method of monitoring parameter optimization in prognostics and health management based on grey clustering decision. Grey Syst.: Theory Appl. **3**, 16–25 (2013)
33. Ye, L., Yunhe, H., Bin, L.: *Study on Adjustment and Optimization Model of Regional Agricultural Structure.* IEEE (2009)
34. Chen, W., Tao, Z., Xiangtao, F., Jinxiu, L.: *Research on Regional Agricultural Structure Optimization Based on Grey Situation Decision Model.* IEEE (2010)
35. Mierzwiak, R.: Selection of the company's strategy using grey stratified decisions mode. In: Series on Grey System. Springer Nature Singapore, pp. 297–312 (2023)
36. Rajesh, R., Aljabhan, B.: A novel grey stratified decision-making (GSDM) model for social sustainability-based supplier selection. IEEE Trans. Comput. Soc. Syst. 1–15 (2022)
37. Deng, J.: Introduction to grey system theory. J. Grey Syst. **1**, 1–24 (1989)
38. Liu, S., Xie, N., Forrest, J.: Novel models of grey relational analysis based on visual angle of similarity and nearness. Grey Syst.: Theory Appl. **1**, 8–18 (2011)
39. Liu, S., Xie, N., Yuan, C., Fang, Z.: *Systems Evaluation: Methods, Models, and Applications.* CRC Press, Boca Raton, London, New York (2011)
40. Konieczny, J.: *Action System Engineering (in Polish).* WNT, Warsaw (1983)
41. Ou, Y.-C.: Using a hybrid decision-making model to evaluate the sustainable development performance of high-tech listed companies. J. Bus. Econ. Manage. **17**(3), 331–346 (2016)
42. Chang, C.-W., Wu, C.-R., Lin, J.-Y.: Multi-approach model for selection of SCMS in semiconductor industry upstream. J. Grey Syst. **20**(2), 135–148 (2008)
43. Gangurde, S.R.: Benchmarking the best factory data collection system (FDC) using AHP-GRA method. Benchmarking **23**(2), 359–370 (2016)
44. Mahdiraji, H.A., Beheshti, M., Jafari-Sadeghi, V., Garcia-Perez, A.: What drives inter-organisational knowledge management? The cause and effect analysis using a multi-layer multi-criteria decision-making framework. J. Knowl. Manage. **26**(9), 2195–2221 (2022)

Correction to: Methodological Aspects of Grey Systems Theory in Management Research

Correction to:
R. Mierzwiak, *Methodological Aspects of Grey Systems Theory in Management Research*, Series on Grey System, https://doi.org/10.1007/978-981-97-2413-0

The original version of the book was inadvertently published with minor errors in Chapters 1, 2 and 4 which have now been corrected. The book and the chapters have been updated with the changes.

The updated versions of these chapters can be found at
https://doi.org/10.1007/978-981-97-2413-0_1
https://doi.org/10.1007/978-981-97-2413-0_2
https://doi.org/10.1007/978-981-97-2413-0_4

R. Mierzwiak, *Methodological Aspects of Grey Systems Theory in Management Research*, Series on Grey System, https://doi.org/10.1007/978-981-97-2413-0_5

The manufacturer's authorised representative in the EU is Springer Nature Customer Service Centre GmbH, Europaplatz 3, 69115 Heidelberg, Germany. If you have any concerns regarding our products, please contact ProductSafety@springernature.com

Printed and bound by CPI Group (UK) Ltd, Croydon, CR0 4YY
01/10/2026
02225876-0007